Singular Moments

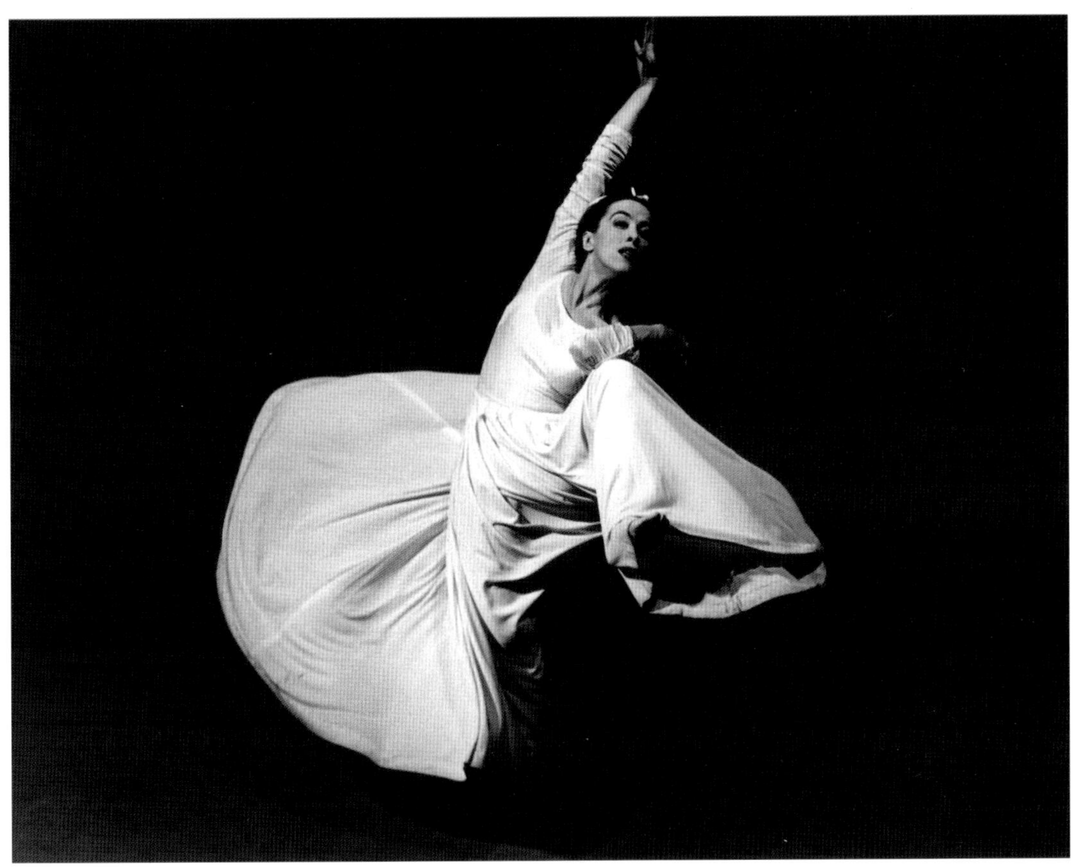

Photographs from the Amon Carter Museum

BY BARBARA McCANDLESS AND JOHN ROHRBACH
WITH SELECT ENTRIES BY HELEN PLUMMER

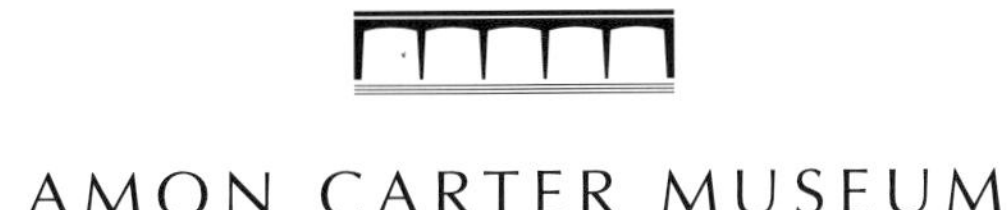

AMON CARTER MUSEUM

The Amon Carter Museum was established through the generosity of Amon G. Carter Sr. (1879–1955) to house his collection of paintings and sculpture by Frederic Remington and Charles M. Russell; to collect, preserve, and exhibit the finest examples of American art; and to serve an educational role through exhibitions, publications, and programs devoted to the study of American art.

Amon Carter Museum
3501 Camp Bowie Boulevard
Fort Worth, Texas 76107-2695
Tel 817.738.1933
Fax 817.377.8523
Web www.cartermuseum.org

FRONT COVER: Harold E. Edgerton and J. Kim Vandiver, *Bullet thru Flame* (detail), 1973

Courtesy of Palm Press, Inc., Gift of James P. Harrington, West Chester, Pennsylvania

TITLE PAGE: Barbara Morgan, *Martha Graham–Letter to the World (Swirl)*, 1940, print 1972
 Gift of the artist

COPYRIGHT PAGE: William H. Rau, *Seneca Coal Breaker, Pittston, Lehigh Valley Railroad* (detail), ca. 1899

BACK COVER: William Henry Jackson, *Tower of Babel, Garden of the Gods* (detail), 1880s

ISBN 0-88360-094-3

Edited by Will Gillham and Peter Keefe
Designed by Keely Edwards
Printed by Cockrell Printing

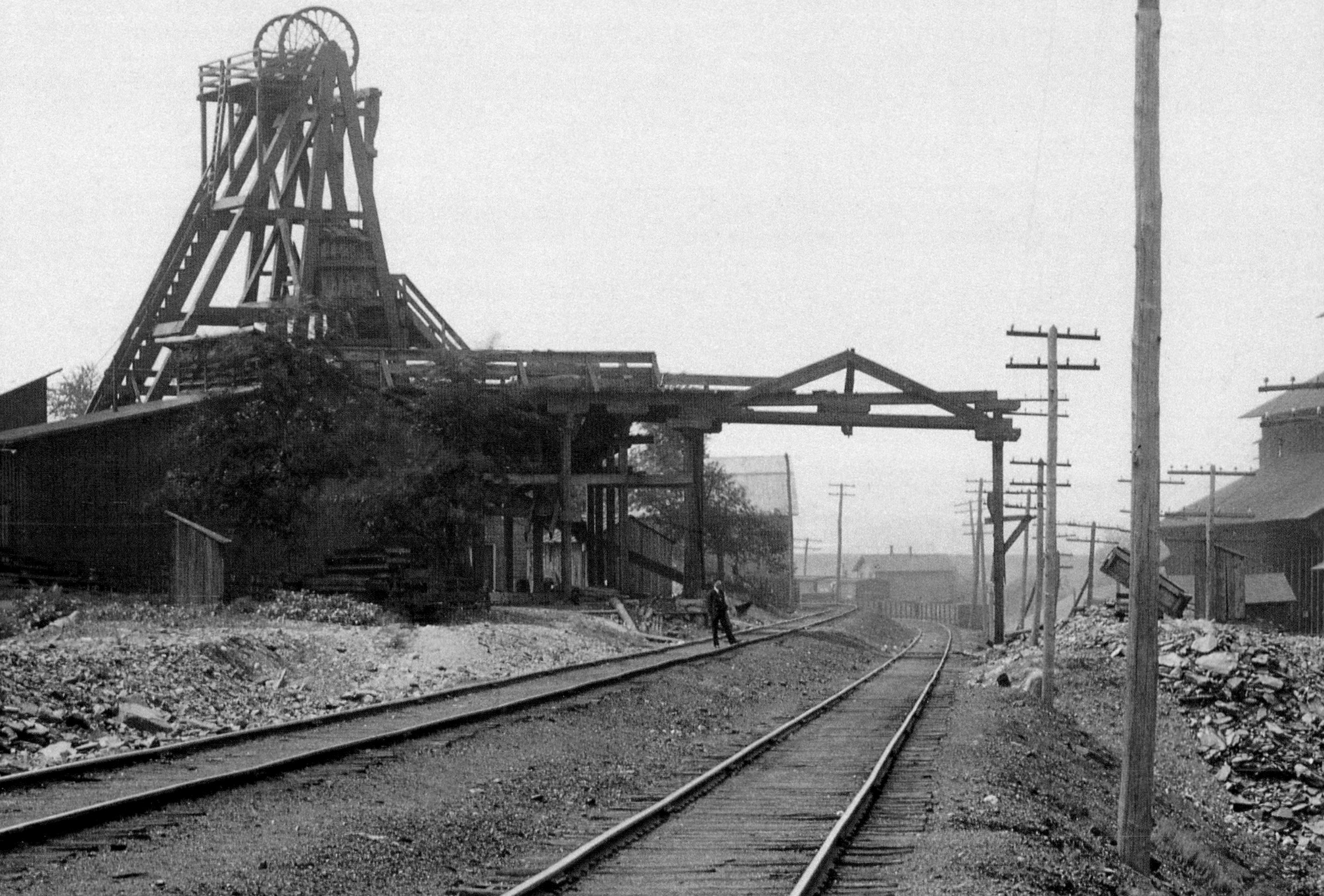

Foreword

Although Amon G. Carter Sr. (1879–1955) did not collect photography, his renowned collection of paintings and sculptures by Frederic Remington and Charles M. Russell, two leading artists of the American West, laid the groundwork for what would become one of the nation's preeminent collections of American photography. While he did not live to see its completion, Carter initiated plans for a museum for the city of Fort Worth; his collection would become the core of the Amon Carter Museum's holdings of American art. Shortly after the museum opened in 1961, photographer Dorothea Lange wrote to Carter's daughter Ruth Carter Stevenson (currently president of the board of trustees). In the mid-1920s, Lange had made some photographs of Charles Russell when he visited her first husband, western painter Maynard Dixon. Since the museum's collection contained so many works by Russell, Lange asked Stevenson if the museum would be interested in having prints of the photographs she had made that day. Thus, Dorothea Lange's interpretive portraits of Charles Russell became the first photographs in the museum's collection.

The museum's first director, Mitchell Wilder, brought to the museum considerable knowledge of fine art photography from his early years as director of the Colorado Springs Fine Arts Center. In the first few years of his directorship at the Carter, he acquired and showcased the work of such leading photographers as Ansel Adams, Edward Weston, and Dorothea Lange. Additionally, with the eager support of Amon G. Carter Jr., a museum trustee and photographer who had learned the art while working for his father's *Fort Worth Star-Telegram*, Wilder advocated that the museum purchase a number of significant groups of photographs while they were still affordable. These insightful acquisitions included a 3,000-print collection of Native American portraits and scenes and a 6,000-piece negative collection of remarkable nineteenth- and twentieth-century portraits from Leavenworth, Kansas. Wilder also supported several photographic survey projects. One of his final acts as director was to commission the celebrated fashion and portrait photographer Richard Avedon, in 1979, to create a portrait of the American West through its people. Although Wilder died later that year, the subsequent 1985 exhibition, *In the American West*, brought national acclaim and attention to the museum's photography collection and educational programs. Under the visionary direction of Wilder, the Carter had become a major resource of both artistic and culturally significant photographs.

Wilder's most lasting legacy, however, may have been his support of photographer Laura Gilpin, which led to the museum becoming the repository of several twentieth-century practitioners. Since his early days in Colorado Springs, Wilder had encouraged Gilpin's lengthy documentary project on the Navajo. After becoming director of the Carter, Wilder introduced Gilpin to the director of the University of Texas Press, who agreed to publish her book *The Enduring Navaho* (1968). That same year, Wilder organized an exhibition to celebrate and publicize the book. In recognition of her friend's early support, Gilpin bequeathed her photographic estate to the Carter. In later years, the museum acquired the archives of photographers Carlotta Corpron, Karl Struss, Erwin Evans Smith, Nell Dorr, and the celebrated nature photographer Eliot Porter.

In 1979 the Carter entered a new phase when Wilder died and Martha Sandweiss began as curator of photographs. The museum formalized what Wilder had begun by broadening the collecting scope from only western art to all types of American art. Charged with expanding the photography collection to fit the museum's objective, just as recognition of the artistic value of photography, among collectors and museums, had caused the prices for fine art photographs to rise dramatically, Sandweiss directed her attention to acquiring individual, rare masterpieces. While adding major works of twentieth-century pictorialism and modernism by such masters as Berenice Abbott and Walker Evans, she continued to acquire key works related to the museum's western strengths. Some of her earliest coups include the first photograph of a Native American, a unique print by the master nineteenth-century landscape photographer Carleton Watkins, and an important collection of daguerreotypes made during the Mexican War, the first photographic depictions of an international conflict.

Throughout the last two decades, the curators have followed their predecessors' examples and continued to acquire masterpieces that clarify the vital role photography has played, and continues to play, in the development and perpetuation of an American art tradition. From its beginnings in 1961, the photography holdings now number over 200,000, and the tripartite collection, comprising fine art photography, historical photography, and artist collections, spans the history of photography in America, from the medium's first appearance in this country in 1840 to the present day. The works on the following pages provide an evocative sampling both of these holdings and of the arresting vitality of the photographic medium.

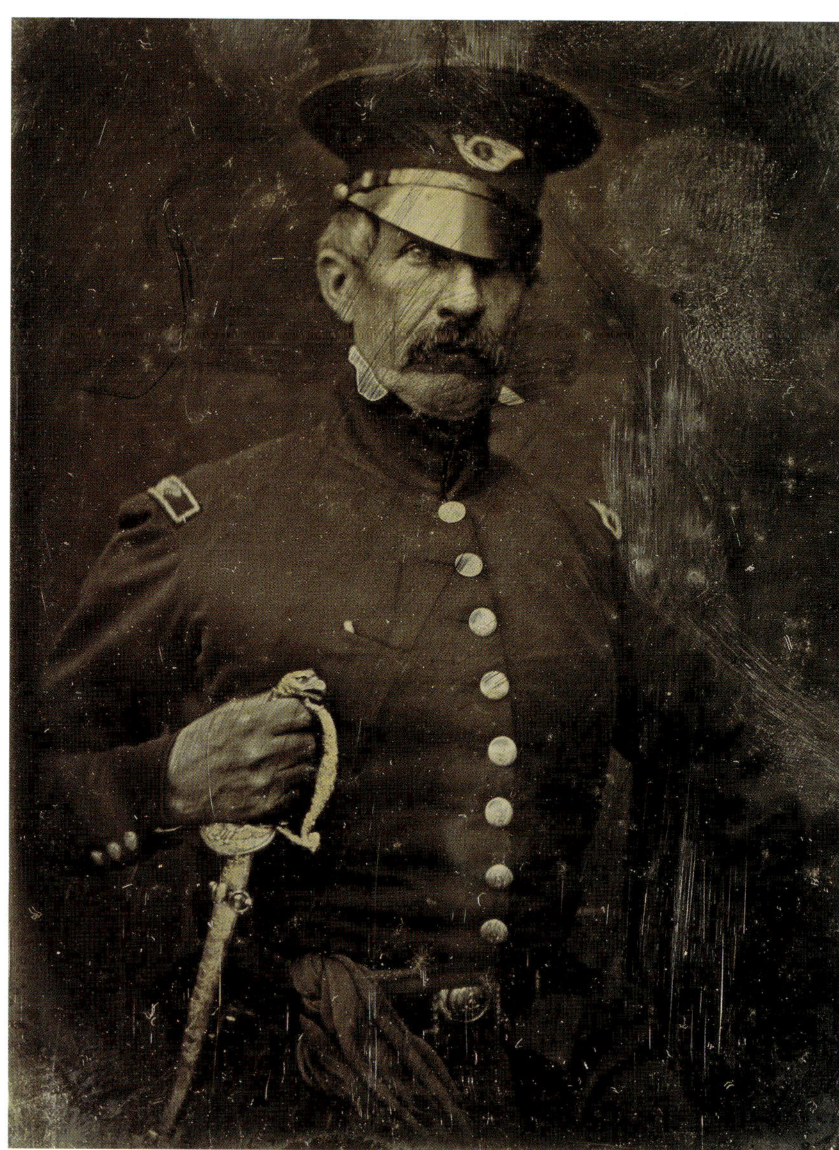

Artist Unknown

Col. Hamtramck, Virginia Volunteers [Colonel John Francis Hamtramck Jr.], ca. 1847
Daguerreotype, quarter plate, with applied color
$4^{1/4}$ x $3^{1/4}$ in. (10.8 x 8.3 cm)
P1981.65.3

Announced in 1839, the first practical photographic process produced daguerreotypes, unique positive images produced on silver-plated sheets of copper. Because daguerreotypes were extremely vulnerable to damage from normal handling, they were usually first covered with a metal mat and then a piece of glass. The entire package was sealed with tape and placed in a protective case. When not handled this way, loose plates, like this one, could become so abraded and tarnished that the image would nearly disappear.

The medium of photography was still in its infancy in 1846 when President Polk signed a declaration of war against Mexico. The U.S.-Mexican War, the first major American conflict fought primarily on foreign soil, was also the first in which war correspondents traveled to the front to report. One such adventure seeker was the unidentified photographer who captured several street scenes in Saltillo and made this portrait of one of the officers stationed there.

Colonel John Hamtramck arrived at General Wool's camp in Buena Vista, Mexico, in August 1847 as commander of the 1st Regiment of Virginia Volunteers. Hamtramck's immediate mission was to resolve discipline and obedience problems. Since military operations in northern Mexico were rare, the boredom with camp routine and frustration with the lack of fighting drove the volunteers to bouts of drunkenness and leaving camp without permission. Hamtramck, a West Point graduate, was respected for his ability to make volunteers as orderly as career soldiers. However, he also apparently delegated too much authority and shirked his responsibilities. After the war ended in June 1848, he led the evacuation and left the less-disciplined troops to bring up the rear. Subsequent reports claimed that the men robbed ranches of livestock and committed atrocities against Mexican civilians. Hamtramck's subordinate, Major Early, endeavored to press charges against him for abandonment of his troops.

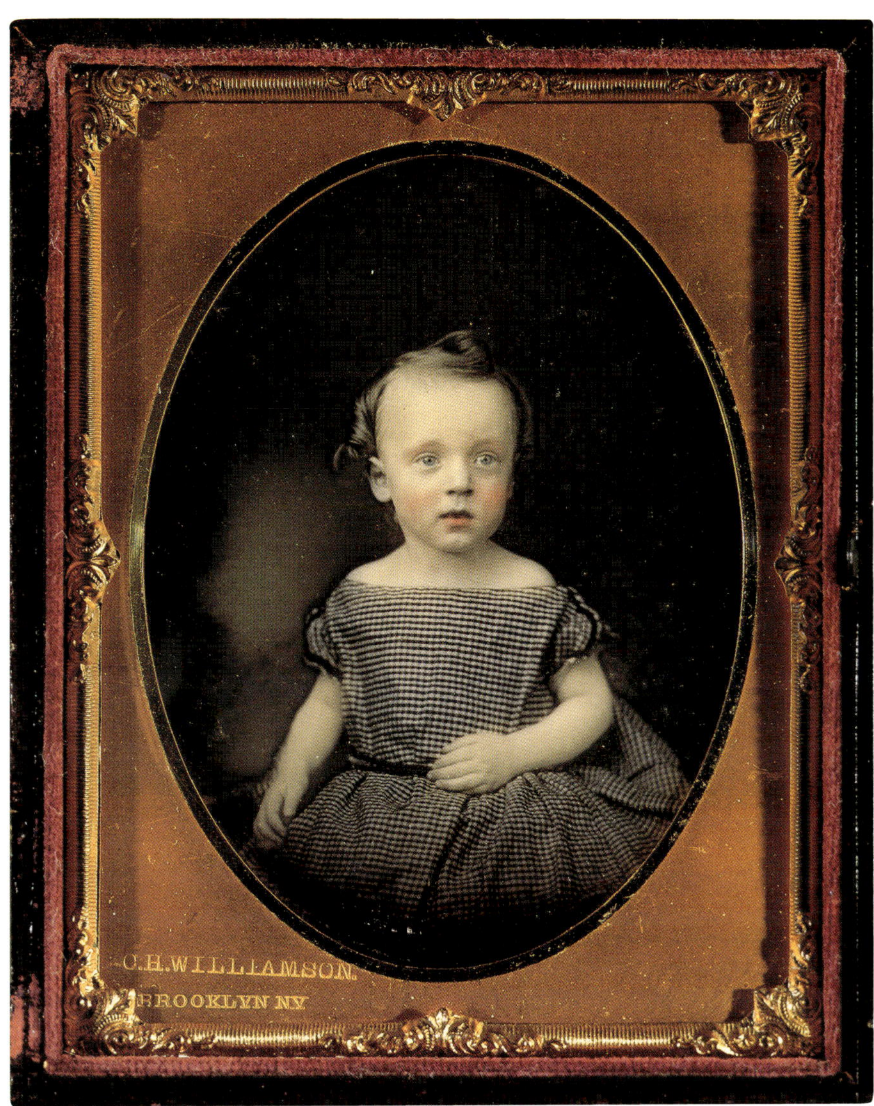

Charles H. Williamson (1826–1874)

[Child wearing checked dress], ca. 1855
Daguerreotype, quarter plate, with applied color
3½ x 2⁹⁄₁₆ in. (8.9 x 6.5 cm)
P1989.22.11

After only a decade of existence, photography was a major industry in America. By 1850 every large town had a daguerreotype studio, with cities like New York, Boston, and Philadelphia having over 100 each. Ten years later, approximately thirty million daguerreotypes had been made, and the vast majority were portraits. One reason for the proliferation of portraits was the high mortality rate and the desire to, as the early advertising slogan said, "secure the shadow, 'ere the substance fades." Children were particularly vulnerable to frequent epidemics of cholera and typhoid, in addition to the normal childhood diseases of measles, mumps, and scarlet fever, and half of all deaths befell children under the age of five.

In 1851 the photographer Charles H. Williamson opened a studio in Brooklyn, where he quickly became known for his sensitive portrayals of children. Williamson had learned the technical intricacies of portraiture by working for such practitioners as Marcus Root and Martin Lawrence. Like most American daguerreotypists, Williamson did not use ornate backdrops. Instead, he used a dark background and lit the sitter as one would a piece of sculpture, creating a three-dimensional effect.

His business thrived, and by 1864 he employed forty people in his studio. Williamson's great success came not only from his specialization with children but also from his talent at hand coloring, most of which he did himself. By applying fine powders to the daguerreotype surface, Williamson could add delicate skin tones and rosy cheeks, resulting in a surprisingly realistic and charming portrait. Curiously, the clothing and hairstyle on this child suggests that the subject was probably a boy rather than a girl. The fashion for children in the 1850s—both boys and girls—was a loose dress or sacque. The only visual clue to gender is often the hairstyle: young girls typically have straight hair parted in the center, while boys wear curled topknots.

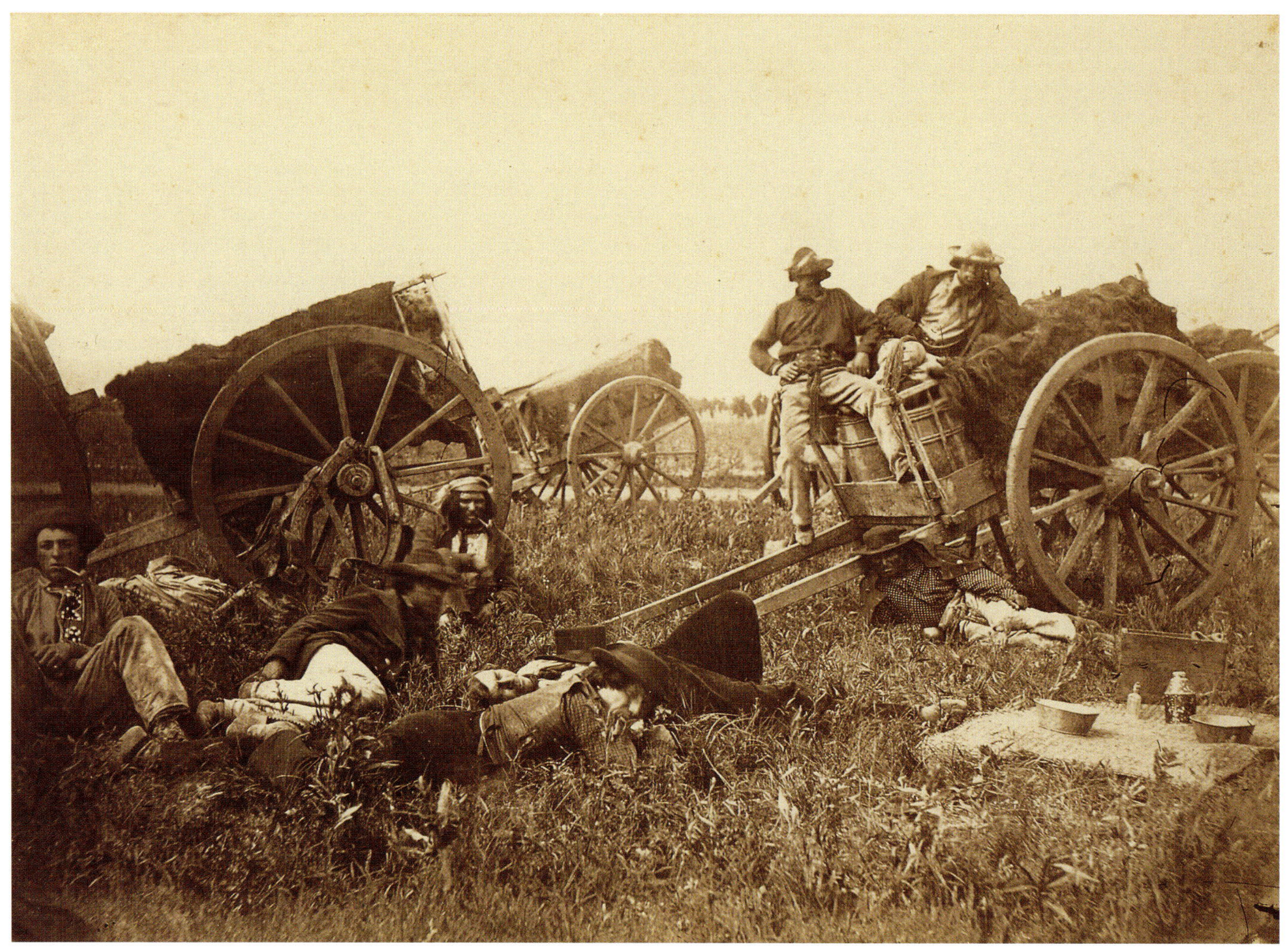

Benjamin F. Upton (1818–after 1901)

Red River Carts, from Pembina, 1858, print ca. 1880
Albumen silver print
6 x 8¼ in. (15.2 x 21 cm)
P1976.19.62

This early photograph of men taking a break while transporting bison furs provides a rare trailside view of the so-called "Red River carts," which were used extensively in the mid-nineteenth century for overland freight on the northern plains. The men appear to be métis, a people of Native American and European heritage common among the seminomadic fur traders who conducted business with Americans in Minnesota and with the British at the Hudson's Bay Company posts farther north. The traders here are likely traveling from the important Pembina trading post on the Canadian border to St. Paul.

Upton, a Maine-born photographer, ran a series of daguerreotype studios in his home state, starting in the mid-1840s, before moving in 1856 to St. Anthony, just north of Minneapolis. There, he took up the collodion glass negative process that was just coming into use. Although this process was cumbersome, necessitating coating, exposing, and developing plates while the collodion was still wet, it allowed multiple prints to be made from the same negative.

Relegating the comforts of studio portrait photography to an assistant, Upton regularly traveled the countryside in a specially equipped darkroom/sleeping wagon seeking out subjects. He produced thousands of photographs, including multiple-print panoramas of St. Anthony, St. Paul, and Minneapolis and views of the Winnebago Agency and Winnebago Indians at their Blue Earth Reservation.

Edward Bromley, a newspaperman and amateur historian, purchased and started reprinting more than 500 of Upton's photographs in 1878. Bromley also interviewed Upton in 1901, learning that he photographed every day the weather was favorable, except Sundays.

George N. Barnard (1819–1902)

Scene of General McPherson's Death, 1864 or 1866
Plate thirty-five from the album *Photographic Views of Sherman's Campaign*
Albumen silver print
10 x 14 in. (25.4 x 36.6 cm)
P1988.25.35

During an engagement on the outskirts of Atlanta on July 22, 1864, thirty-five-year-old Union Army General James Birdseye McPherson was surveying a section of the Union line that he thought was under his troops' control. Suddenly he came face-to-face with a group of Confederate infantrymen. Ignoring their orders to surrender, he wheeled his horse around to gallop off through the dense forest only to be struck in the back by a bullet. He died within minutes.

Barnard had met and photographed the popular and respected general earlier that year and likely had gone to see his funeral procession as it worked its way from Georgia back to his Clyde, Ohio, hometown. When called to Atlanta that September to document the grisly aftermath of General William Tecumseh Sherman's capture of that city, Barnard made a special trip to the site of McPherson's death. On that occasion and during a subsequent visit, he made a series of photographs, including this macabre epitaph. To achieve this haunting view, Barnard darkened the trunk of the central tree in order to draw one's eye to the horse bones and skull he had arranged at the foot of the tree to the left. He may even have added the cannonballs splayed across the small clearing. These adjustments effectively organize and naturalize the scene, creating a stagelike composition built upon powerful symbols of the war.

Barnard drew on more than fifteen years of photographic experience to create this work. He began his career making daguerreotypes in Oswego, New York, in 1847. He joined Mathew Brady's Washington, D.C., gallery in time to photograph Abraham Lincoln's inauguration. He photographed battle sites for Brady and Alexander Gardner before being hired to run the photographic operations of the U.S. Army's Department of Engineers. Hoping to capitalize on the wave of interest in Sherman's campaign in 1866, Barnard privately published a sixty-one-plate album of original prints commemorating the event. This image comes from the Amon Carter Museum's splendid copy of that album.

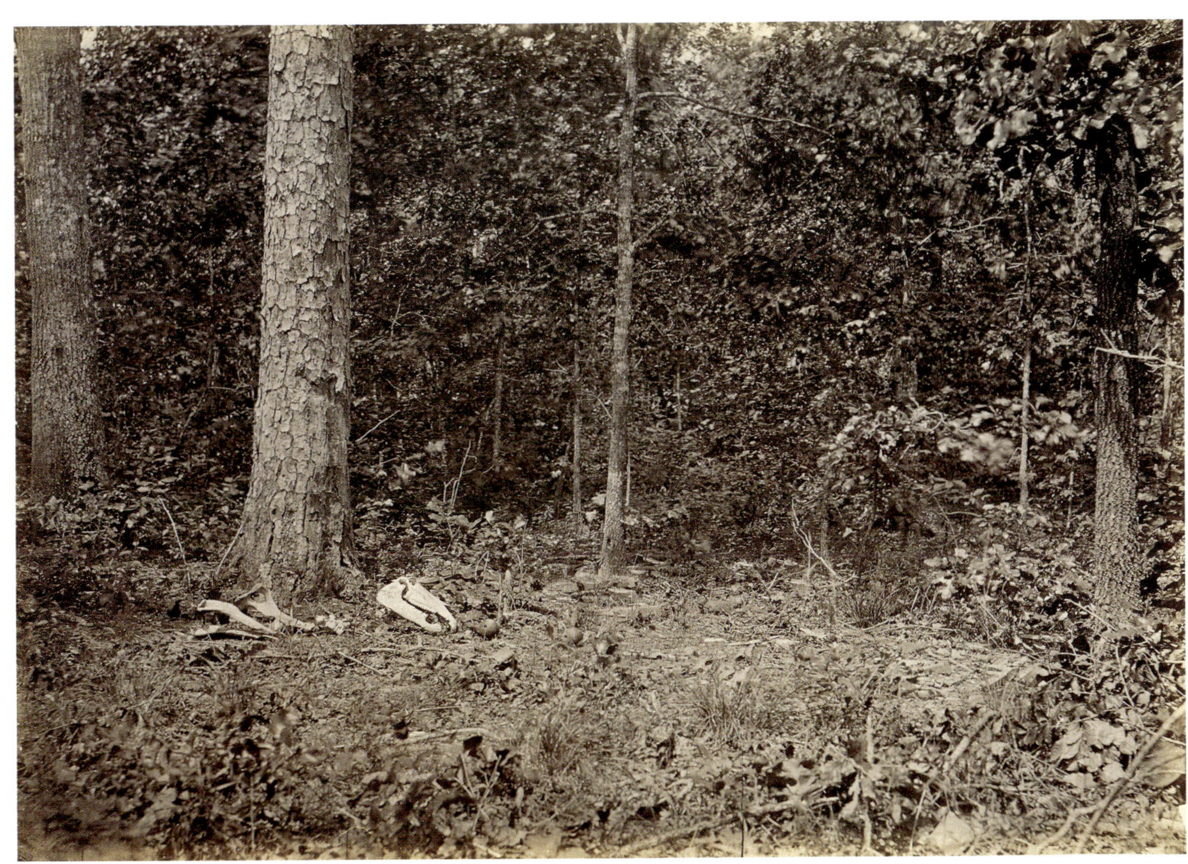

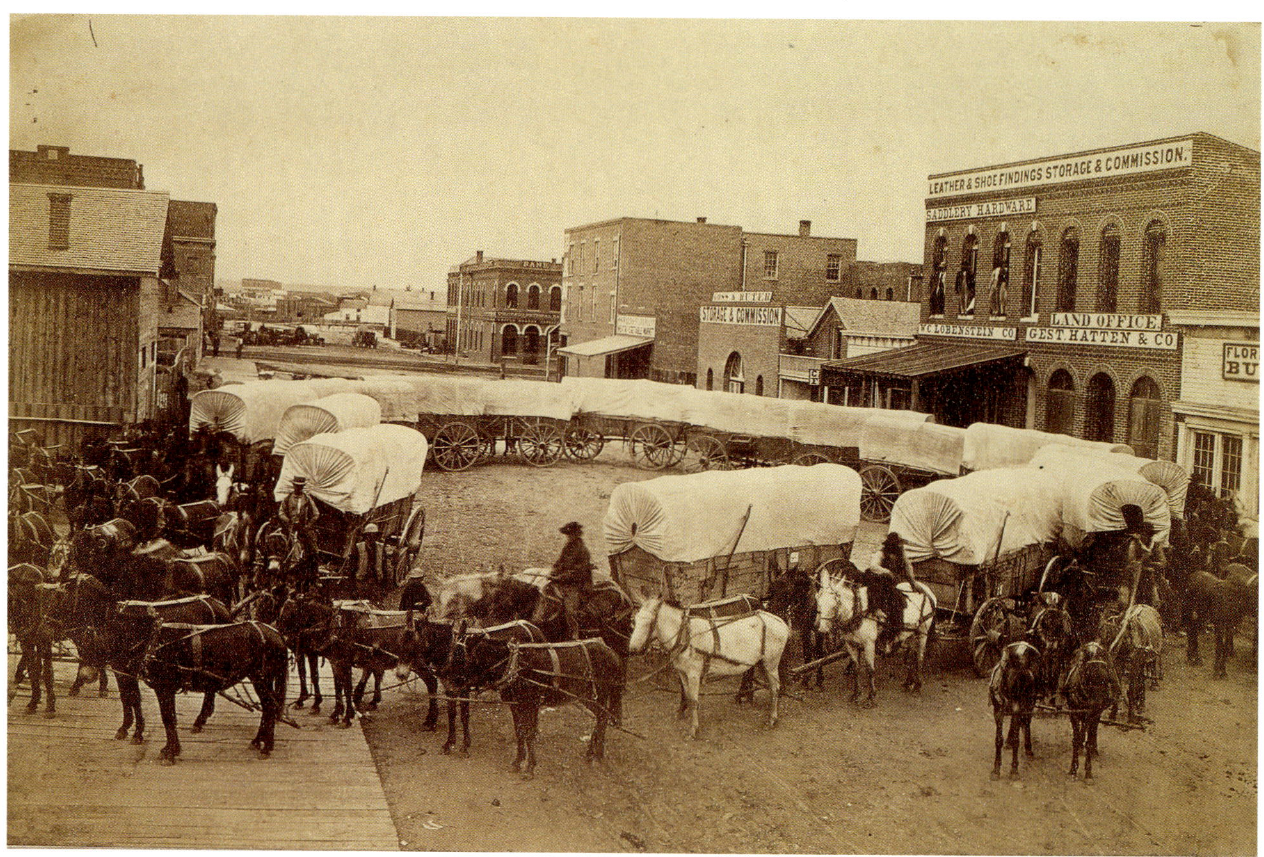

William G. Chamberlain (1815–1910)

Street Scene in Denver, 1868
Albumen silver print
$5\frac{1}{2}$ x 8 in. (14 x 20.3 cm)
P1976.3.3

The brick buildings lining this June 1868 view of Market Street in Denver evoke a sense of prosperous stability. Despite contending with fires, floods, and continuing conflicts with surrounding Plains Indians, the city was fast becoming a freight center and launching point for those lured into the surrounding mountains by discoveries of gold. The supply train depicted here was owned by David Bruce Powers, who ran a regular route between Leavenworth, Kansas, and Denver until the completion of rail lines to the city in 1870.

Powers and his crew may have rounded up the Conestoga wagons across the middle of the street solely to get their photograph made. Yet, this remarkable arrangement aptly symbolizes travelers' fears of being attacked by Cheyenne raiders on their way across the plains. Indeed, when Powers' drovers hired themselves out to cut and haul hay after unloading their supplies, they were attacked by Indians, who killed or drove off all their mules. Powers subsequently applied to the government for reimbursement, but his claim was refused because the train was not on its regular route.

William G. Chamberlain had stopped in Denver with his family in 1860 while enroute to settling in California. Finding that the Colorado climate greatly improved his wife's health, he decided to stay. The photographer ran a series of portrait studios in Denver and Central City, Colorado, between 1861 and 1881. Besides documenting activities like this freight supply train, he regularly assembled views of towns and mountain scenery for sale as inexpensive mementos of the region. In 1881 he sold his studio to take up an early form of halftone book illustration.

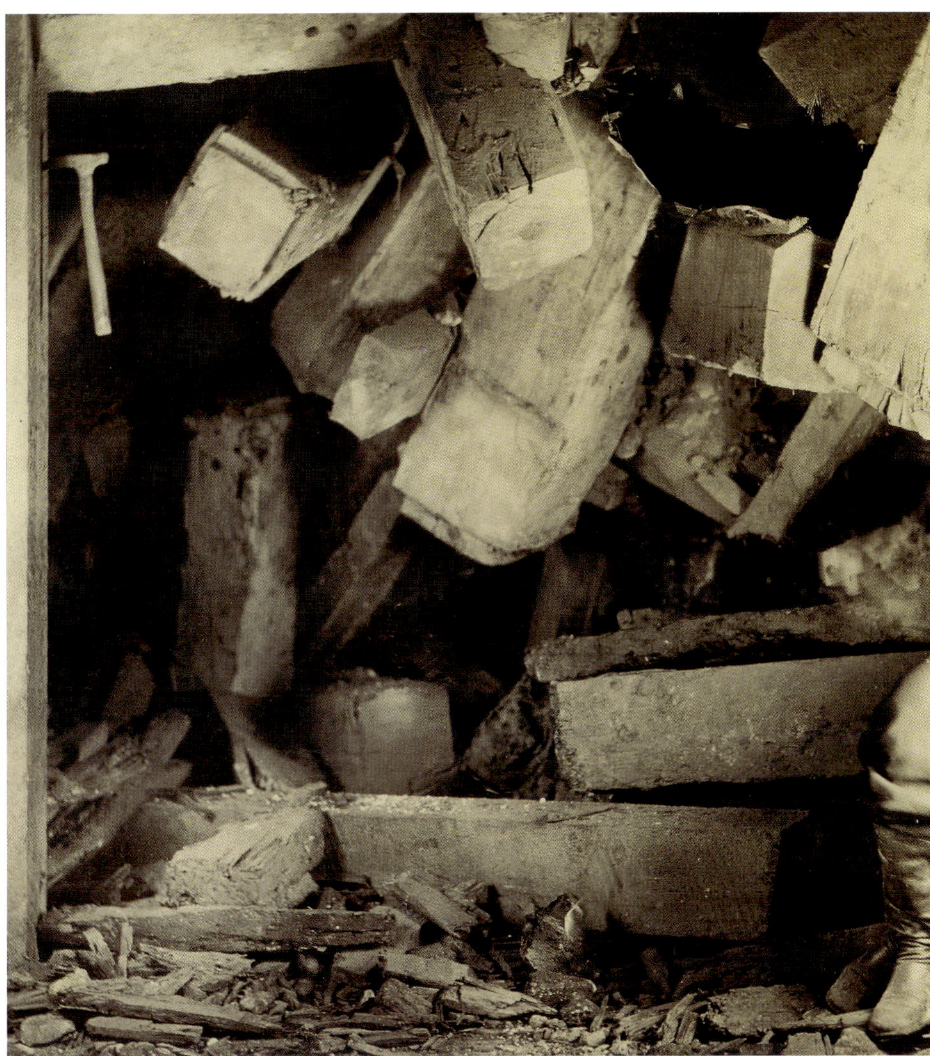

Timothy H. O'Sullivan (1840–1882)

Cave-in at Comstock Mine, Virginia City, Nevada, 1868
Albumen silver print
6¾ x 6 in. (17.1 x 15.2 cm)
P1991.4.2

In spring 1867 the U.S. Army's Department of Engineers organized an expedition to survey the topography, geology, and natural resources along the fortieth parallel between the California/Nevada border and Denver. The survey's mandate included detailing the economic potential of the land along the proposed routes of the Central Pacific and Union Pacific Railroads. Twenty-five-year-old Clarence King, a geologist who had worked the previous four years on the California Geological Survey, led the explorations. Timothy O'Sullivan, having gained extensive photographic experience during the Civil War working for Mathew Brady and Alexander Gardner, became the expedition's photographer.

During its first season, the King Survey, as it came to be known, explored much of western Nevada. But in early 1868, before heading to southern Idaho and on to Salt Lake City, O'Sullivan visited the gold and silver mines around Virginia City, Nevada. There, he made the earliest known photographs of mine interiors, including this vivid record of a cave-in at the Gould and Curry Mine. The tangle of huge, crushed timbers gives an immediate sense of claustrophobia to the collapse. The pick driven into the beam at the upper left and the booted legs intruding at the lower right add further poignancy. The booted man is likely holding O'Sullivan's magnesium flash. But his cropped legs and the mining pick offer vivid, disturbing suggestions of the men that were likely crushed by the beams.

O'Sullivan worked for King one more summer before traveling to Panama's Isthmus of Darien to document a navy expedition searching for a canal route. He joined Lt. George Wheeler's government-sponsored survey of southern Nevada and Utah the following year and in 1872 returned to work for King. He then spent two more years with the Wheeler survey before going into business on his own. In 1880 he was appointed photographer of the Treasury Department, but he died of tuberculosis shortly thereafter.

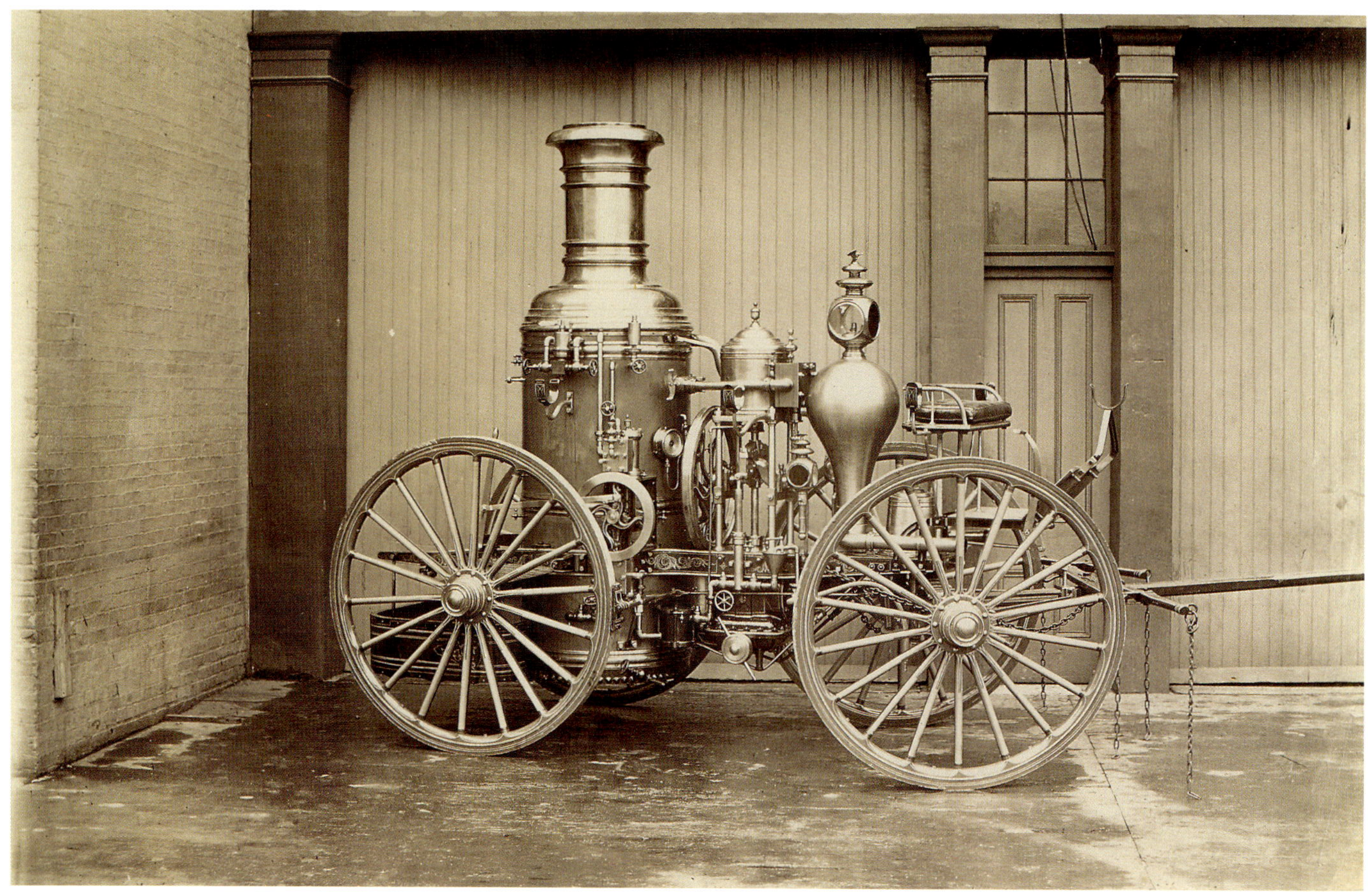

Artist Unknown

Fire Engine, Cincinnati, Ohio, 1870
Albumen silver print
11 x 17 in. (27.9 x 43.2 cm)
P1990.8

Fire engines and fire scenes were popular nineteenth-century genre subjects. But this photograph was likely created as a simple product shot by the company that built this engine. Such photographs provided a common means for sharing detailed information about large vehicles and heavy machinery. Even so, this image's exceptional condition and size make it a potent symbol of America's age of steam.

Cincinnati was the first city to fully adopt steam fire engines, and it was here in 1853 that Alexander B. Latta produced the first truly successful design for such a vehicle. Cincinnati also established the first professional fire department. But not everyone favored these developments. Just as clipper ship captains competed with steam vessels, many firefighters initially preferred the hand pumper. They surely cheered in 1855 when a powerful hand engine won a close race at City Hall Park in New York City against one of Latta's steamers. But they also must have recognized the relentless stamina and efficiency provided by steam power.

The vehicle shown here, based on a Latta design, documents the beginning of the shift from hand-pulled to horse-drawn carts. The elaborately painted wheels also reflect the pride that firemen took, and still take, in the appearance of their machines.

Carleton E. Watkins (1829–1916)

Malakoff Diggins, North Bloomfield, Nevada County, 1871
Albumen silver print
$16^{3}/_{8}$ x $21^{1}/_{2}$ in. (41.6 x 54.6 cm)
P1989.13.4

The discovery of ancient riverbeds far below the surface of the ground opened up exciting new prospects for mining in northern California, but these ventures required a considerable financial investment to make them profitable. Using a technique called hydraulic mining, a powerful stream of water was directed at the earth, breaking the rock into gravel that could be easily worked. When this image was made, the North Bloomfield Gravel Mining Company was conducting the largest hydraulic mining operation in the state but had just discovered that the top gravel would not yield enough ore to recoup its already huge investment. Instead, more money would be needed to construct a tunnel to carry water and debris downstream.

To help attract English investors to support the project, the company hired San Francisco photographer Carleton Watkins. His photographs were successful in attracting investors, but in 1882 farmers whose lands were flooded by the mud washing downstream brought suit against the mining company in what was the first environmental court case.

Watkins, widely considered among the most accomplished of nineteenth-century American landscape photographers, is best known for his magnificent views of the Yosemite Valley wilderness. But he made his living as a commercial photographer who excelled at constructing a visual language that perfectly conveyed his client's message. Adept at using foreground and background details to compose the image, Watkins here selected a vantage point that placed the cabin on the left side of the ridge within the earthen spires left behind by the pressurized water. The viewer then compares all other pictorial elements to the cabin to achieve a sense of scale. The pipeline in the foreground delivering water to the operation seems massive in comparison, while the opening in the ridge reveals the arcing streams of water in the distant background that have washed away the hillside. The enormous crater left behind thus communicates the effectiveness of such an operation in carving away the landscape, all in the service of industry.

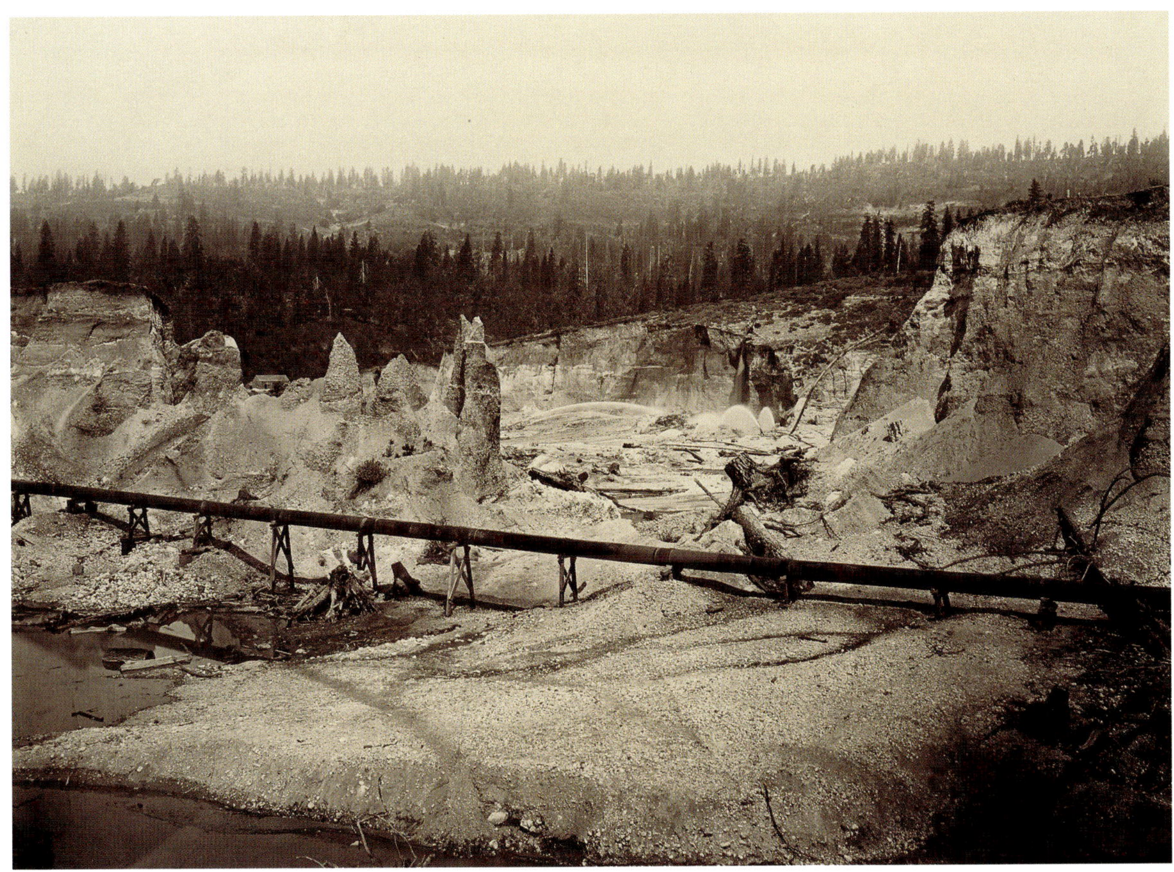

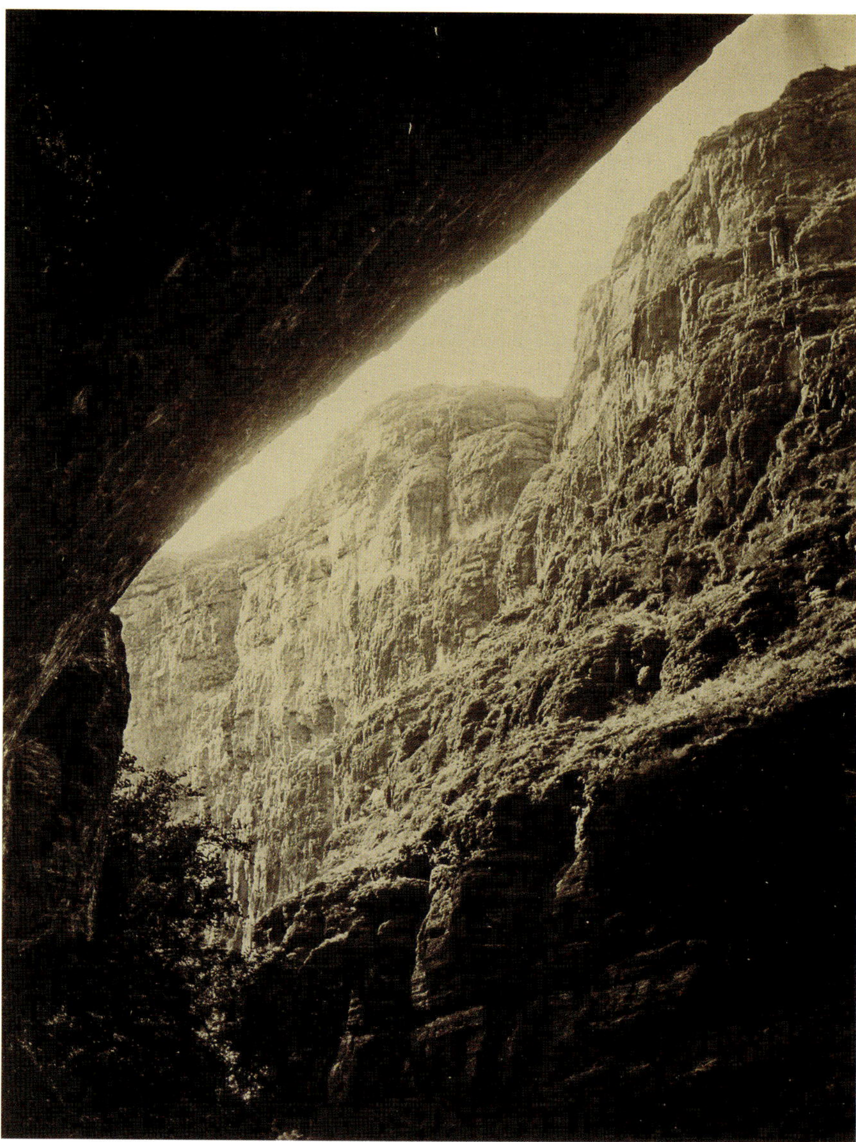

William Bell
(1830–1910)

Canon of Kanab Wash, Colorado River, Looking South, 1872
Section two, plate four, from the album
Geographical Explorations and Surveys West of the 100th Meridian — Wheeler Photographs
Albumen silver print
10⅝ x 8 in. (27 x 20.3 cm)
P1982.27.20

"The lover of nature, whose perceptions have been trained in the Alps, in Italy, Germany, or New England, in the Appalachians or Cordilleras, in Scotland or Colorado, would enter this strange region with a shock, and dwell there for a time with a sense of oppression, and perhaps with horror." So said the geologist Clarence Dutton in his 1882 study of the Grand Canyon. The magnificent, oversized terrain of the Colorado River plateau contains the largest concentration of national parks and monuments in the contiguous United States.

Realizing that photographs raised invaluable public support, Lt. George M. Wheeler hired the Philadelphia photographer William Bell in 1872 to join his continuing, military-sponsored reconnaissance through northern Arizona and southern Utah. Bell brought an eye for drama to the expedition, taking advantage of the traverse of the Grand Canyon to create some of the most compelling photographic portraits of the inner gorges ever produced.

Clarence Dutton would have appreciated this forbidding vision of the massive, bleak cliffs of Kanab Wash. The image exudes an aura of desolation and impending doom. Its slit of brilliant, hot sky amplifies the darkened recesses of the magnificent side canyon, which opens into the heart of the Grand Canyon's north side. Although the tree in the lower left is a symbol of life and provides scale, the overhanging wall dominates the scene, delivering a sense that one might be crushed at any moment under its weight. One year working in these difficult conditions was enough for Bell.

In subsequent years the government printed and presented Bell's 1872 photographs in exhibitions both in the United States and Europe and also published a magnificent album of fifty tipped-in photographs taken by Bell and photographer Timothy O'Sullivan on Wheeler's 1871–73 surveys of the region. This image is taken from the Amon Carter Museum's complete collection of the fifty images.

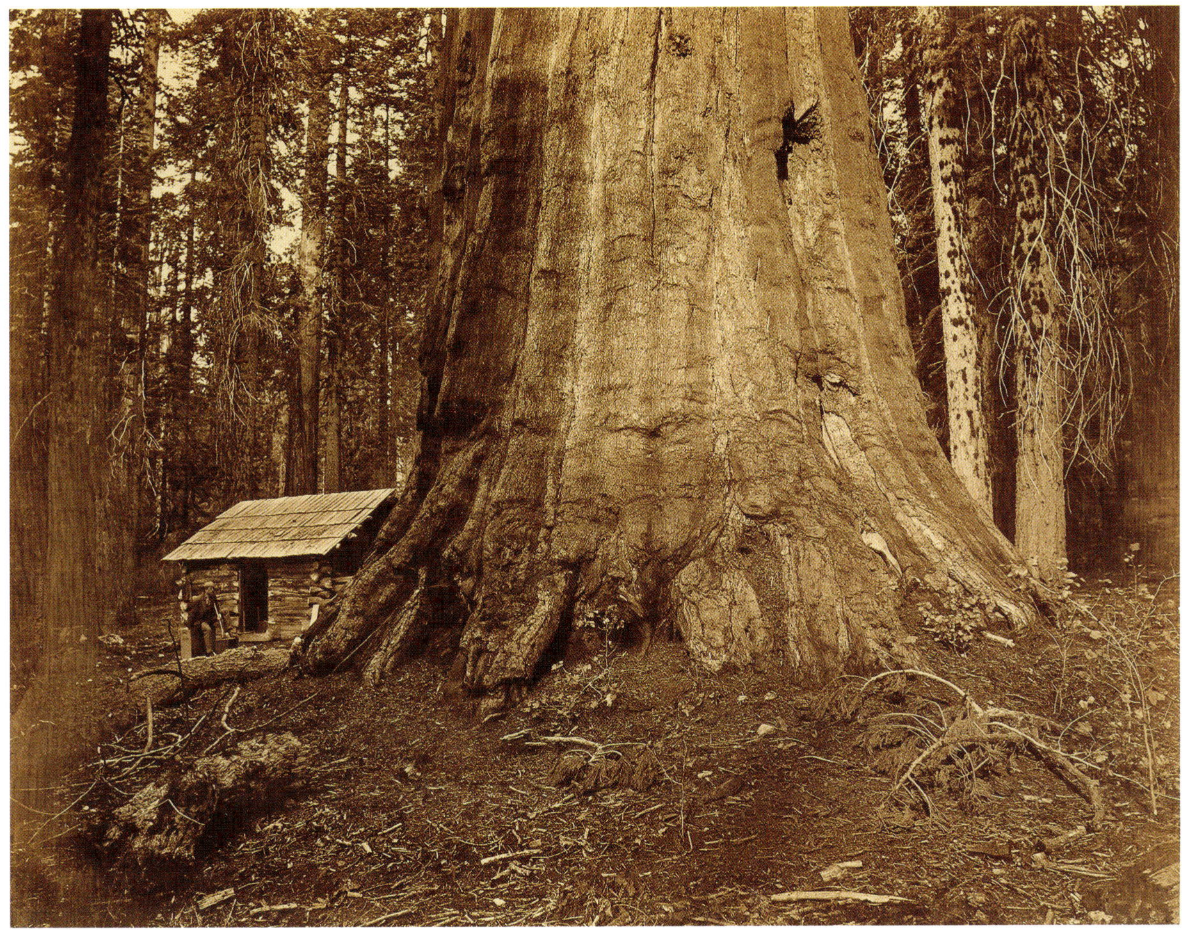

Eadweard Muybridge (1830–1904)

Mariposa Grove of Mammoth Trees. Wm H. Seward, 85 Feet in Circumference, 268 Feet High, 1872
Albumen silver print
16 7/8 x 21 5/16 in. (42.9 x 54.1 cm)
P1972.32.5

The big trees of California were first discovered in 1852, when a hunter following a bear stumbled upon one of the groves. The area soon became a favorite destination for tourists and, in 1859, the first photographs of the area were made. Both Charles Leander Weed and Carleton Watkins received critical acclaim for their mammoth-plate views (produced with eighteen-by-twenty-two-inch glass negatives) taken in the Yosemite area during the 1860s. These views helped convince Congress to protect the valley and the Mariposa Grove through the Yosemite Act of 1864.

These majestic trees, some as old as 4,000 years, gave America the sense of symbolic history it had been lacking, and Californians began to name the trees after important American statesmen and writers. The tree in this view bears the name of William H. Seward, secretary of state from 1861–69 under both Abraham Lincoln and Andrew Johnson. Galen Clark, the guardian of the Yosemite Grant, built the log cabin at the base of this tree as a shelter for the growing number of travelers; it soon became known as "Galen's Hospice."

Eadweard Muybridge's first views of the area in 1867—although modest in size—were praised at the time for being artistically superior to those made by both Weed and Watkins. But in keeping with those predecessors, Muybridge returned to the valley in 1872 with a mammoth-plate camera. One of the many sponsors of his venture was the painter Albert Bierstadt, whom Muybridge had met earlier that year at a reception for the San Francisco Art Association. The two traveled to the valley together that summer, and Bierstadt advised the photographer on his aesthetic compositions. In late fall, on his way back to San Francisco, Muybridge visited the Mariposa Grove and made one final mammoth-plate view. To convey the impressive scale of the tree, Muybridge concentrated on the base, filling the frame with the massive trunk and dwarfing the figure and cabin.

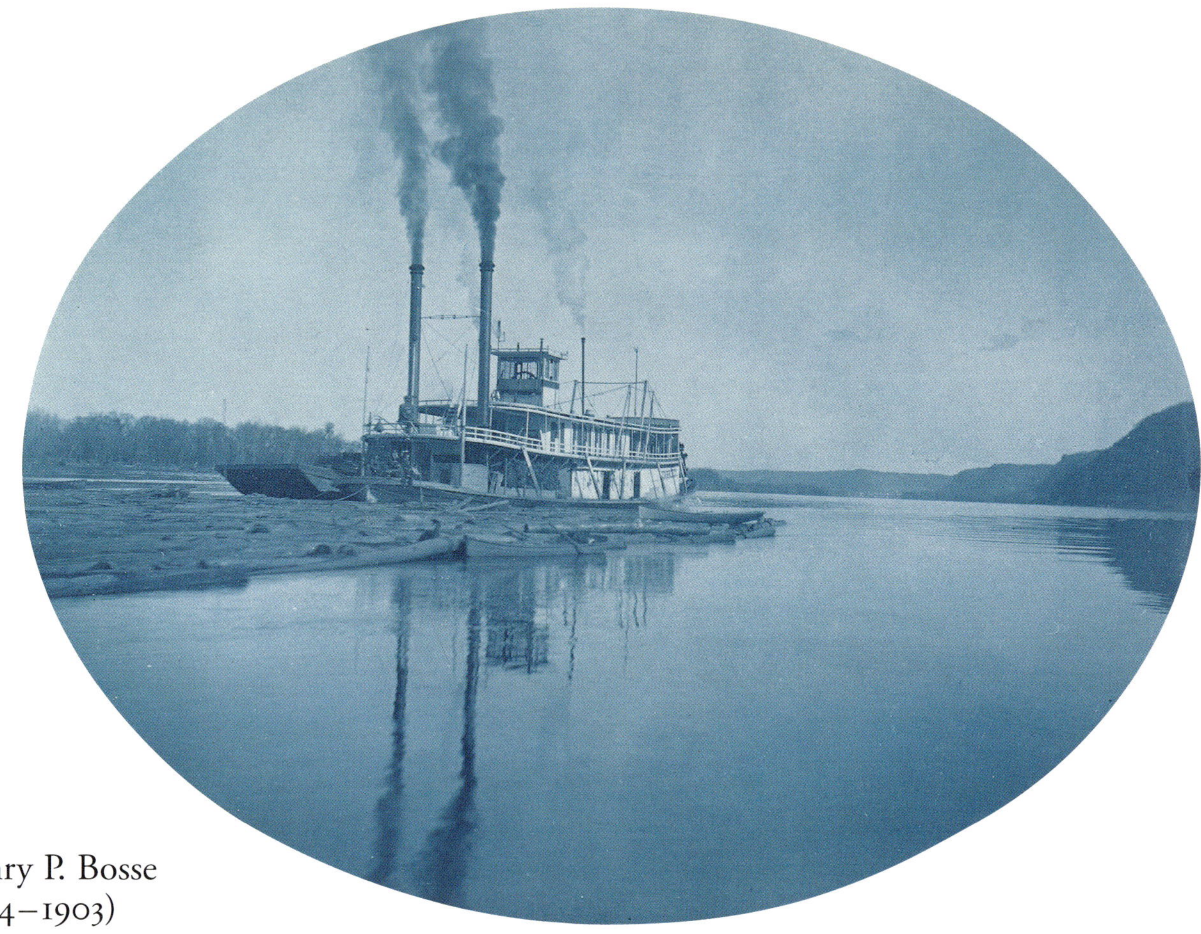

Henry P. Bosse (1844–1903)

Raftboat "Ten Brook," 1885
Plate 169, from the album *Views on the Upper Mississippi River*
Cyanotype
10⅝ x 13½ in. (27 x 34.3 cm)
P1997.49

Flood control and shifting channels along the Mississippi River have long been an issue of regional and national debate. In 1879 Congress established the Mississippi River Commission, charging it to develop a comprehensive plan to improve navigation on the river. When the commission subsequently gave the U.S. Army Corps of Engineers responsibility to make the necessary improvements, the corps began an eight-year project to establish a permanent, four-and-one-half-foot-deep channel between St. Louis and Minneapolis by dredging the river and building wing and closing dams designed to quicken the river's flow.

As chief draftsman in the Rock Island, Illinois, office of the Corps of Engineers during these years, Henry Bosse was given the task of documenting the corps' work. Besides photographing the dams and dredging operations, Bosse turned his camera on the towns, cities, bridges, and countryside that lined the Mississippi's banks, using his images to refine his map of the river. He also took occasional shots of river traffic, including this picturesque view of a steamboat pushing logs downriver. Taken together, these views chronicle the first systematic effort to transform the Mississippi from a natural river into a modern commercial highway.

Although little is known about Bosse, he apparently studied art in Germany before immigrating to the United States in 1865. That art training is clearly evident in his meticulous compositions, attention to lighting, oval image framing, and choice of the cyanotype over the more standard albumen and gelatin silver processes. Atmosphere and crystalline light pervade this view of the *Ten Brook*, establishing a mood of restful contemplation. Yet this peaceful mood is carefully balanced with the river's commerce, so essential to America's rapidly evolving economy.

Upon completion of his photographic project, Bosse assembled a small group of presentation albums, each holding 169 unusually large and finely printed cyanotypes. (Only four copies have been located.) This print comes from the album that was owned by Bosse's supervisor, Major Alexander MacKenzie.

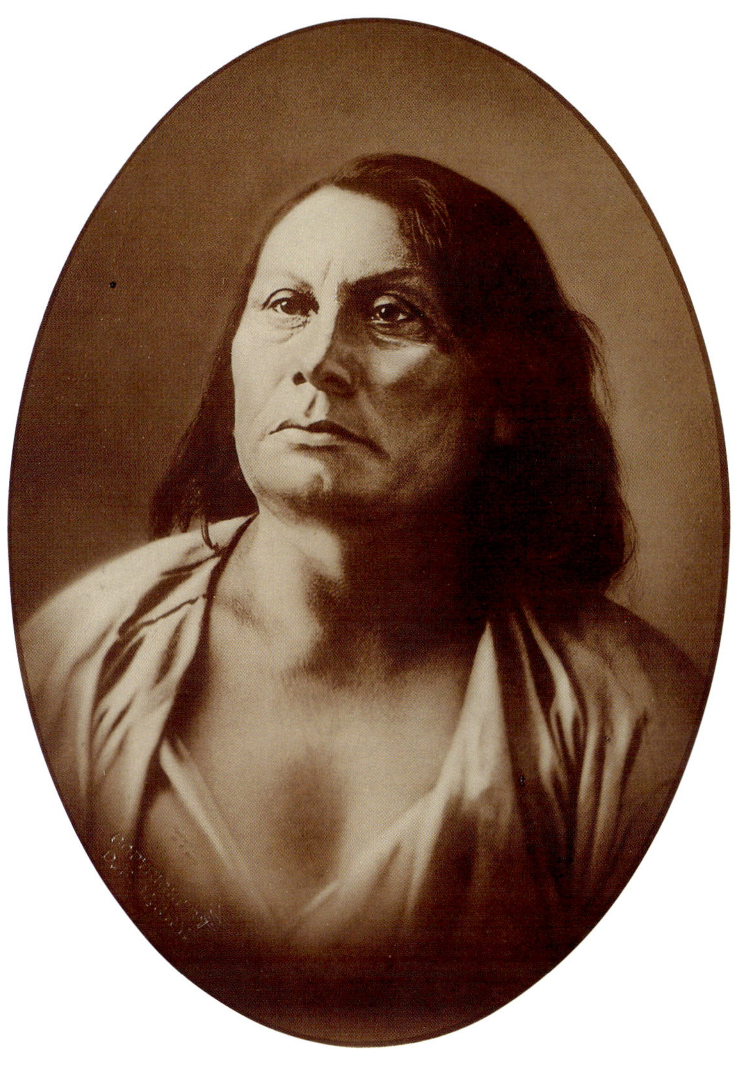

David Francis Barry (1854–1934)

Chief Gall or Pizi, ca. 1886, print after 1894
Collodion chloride print
7½ x 5 in. (19.0 x 12.7 cm)
P1967.464

Enterprising twenty-one-year-old photographer David Barry arrived in the Dakota Territory in 1875, just after gold was discovered in the Black Hills. He settled at Fort Abraham Lincoln, near present day Bismarck. For the next fifteen years, the combination of his winning personality and photographic skills resulted in his systematic creation of many extraordinary images. Military men, such as General George A. Custer, frontier guides, and the indigenous populations were all subjects for Barry's portraits. Depictions of notable Sioux, like Sitting Bull, who became his friend, greatly contributed to Barry's success in the East as a freelance photographer.

By the mid-1880s, "Barry's Photograph Parlor" was a luxurious studio in Bismarck. Even so, the charismatic artist frequently traveled to surrounding forts to play poker with friends, document personalities in natural light, and take advantage of other photographic opportunities. One such opportunity presented itself on the tenth anniversary of the Battle of the Little Bighorn, June 25, 1886. While standing beside the graves of Custer's command, Hunkpapa Chief Gall both spoke about and pantomined the events of a decade earlier to a silent crowd. Present that day, in addition to Barry, were many Sioux, Cheyenne, and U.S. military men who, in 1876, had participated in the thirty-five minute battle. Gall's achievements as a warrior verged on the legendary, and he had won respect as a brilliant strategist and field commander for Sitting Bull. By the mid-1880s, though, reservation life had become a reality for nearly all Sioux. Barry probably created this image on or near the Standing Rock Reservation around the time of the 1886 reunion.

In this remarkable portrait, Chief Gall shows unmistakable confidence and an authoritative nature. Unlike most of Barry's subjects, Gall refused the photographer's instructions on how to pose for the camera. With his uncharacteristic, free-flowing hair, a sign of humility before the Great Spirit, and exposed chest devoid of robes or adornment, the chief appears ready for battle. Barry's interpretation of Gall so impressed Mrs. Elizabeth Custer that she wrote in a letter, "Mr. Barry, as painful as it is for me to look upon the pictured face of an Indian, I never dreamed in all my life that there could be in all the tribes so fine a specimen for a warrior as Chief Gall."

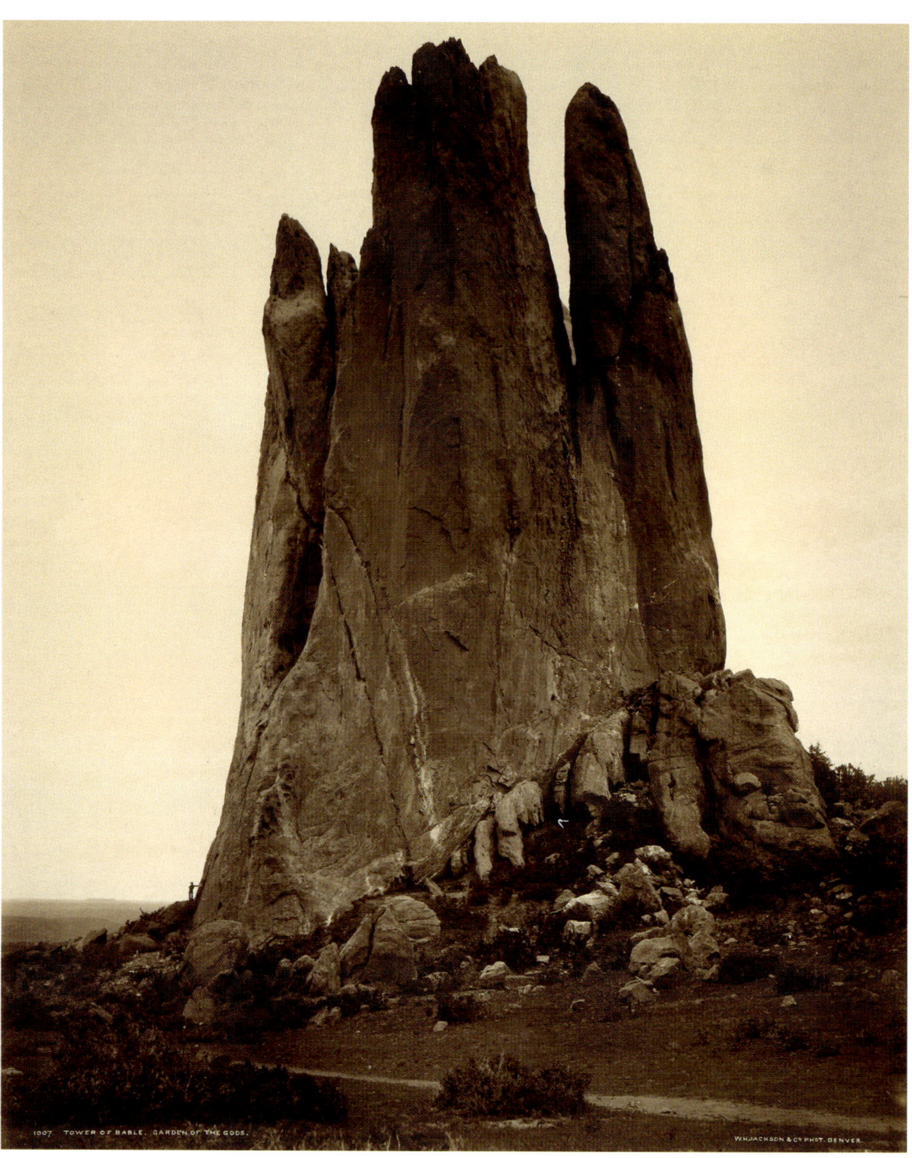

William Henry Jackson (1843–1942)

Tower of Babel, Garden of the Gods, 1880s
Albumen silver print
21¼ x 17 in. (54 x 43.2 cm)
P1981.47.2

Denver had emerged as a major rail hub, financial center, and health spa when William Henry Jackson chose to settle there and set up a studio in 1879. Having gained extensive knowledge of the region's terrain in the 1870s while photographing for Ferdinand V. Hayden's U.S. Geological and Geographical Survey of the Territories, Jackson now set about turning the region into a tourist destination.

Almost immediately, he gained an extensive commission to photograph for the Denver and Rio Grande Railroad, a local company that proclaimed itself "the scenic line of America." While Jackson's photographs were initially meant to provide the basis for promotional illustrations by his friend, the painter Thomas Moran, his extraordinary mammoth-plate prints were an immediate success. Over the next twelve years, each time the railroad opened a new section of track, Jackson was hired to create scenic views of the stretch. To facilitate the photographer's work, the railroad often provided him with his own train and customized darkroom/parlor car so he could stop whenever, wherever, and for however long he wished. The resulting prints decorated the region's rail stations and were sold to tourists.

Jackson may have created this large, elegantly composed study of the famous sandstone Tower of Babel for sale by his own Denver-based photograph and publishing company. By this time his sphere of operations was expanding to include much of the United States and even Mexico. The diminutive figure posed at the left side of the base of the rock reveals the tower's monumental proportions. The foreground path reflects the site's easy accessibility and popularity. Such photographs both persuaded viewers to travel to these "playgrounds" and became valued mementos of their excursions.

William H. Rau (1855–1920)

Seneca Coal Breaker, Pittston, Lehigh Valley Railroad, ca. 1899
Albumen silver print
17¼ x 20½ in. (43.8 x 52.1 cm)
P1991.5

While the West was being transformed into a vast tourist attraction, the East was fast becoming a concentrated network of urban and corporate industrialism. Pittston, a northeastern Pennsylvania steel town whose operations depended on the regular arrival of thousands of coal cars running on the track of the Lehigh Valley Railroad (LVRR), was firmly enmeshed in that web.

William Rau gained his early training in the West making Rocky Mountain views and working briefly for William Henry Jackson. In 1885 he returned to Philadelphia to set up a studio, and he photographed prolifically in and around southeastern Pennsylvania. By this date, railroads knew the value of publicity photographs detailing both their activities and the scenic wonders along their routes. Therefore, it is not surprising that the Pennsylvania Railroad hired Rau in 1890 for just that purpose, providing him with a comfortable darkroom/parlor car, much like the one used by Jackson in Colorado. Rau's work for the Pennsylvania Railroad, including his production of a number of eighteen-by-forty-seven-inch panoramas, was so admired that the LVRR hired him to make similar views.

Between 1895 and the turn of the century, Rau made hundreds of large photographs of both the scenic landscape and important industrial sites along the LVRR's track, following the line from New York City down Pennsylvania's Lehigh Valley and up through New York State to Niagara Falls. In the process, he created some of his most significant photographs, including this remarkable view of a massive coal breaker in the rail line town of Pittston. The company eventually framed more than 200 of these views, placing them in public spaces as far west as Chicago.

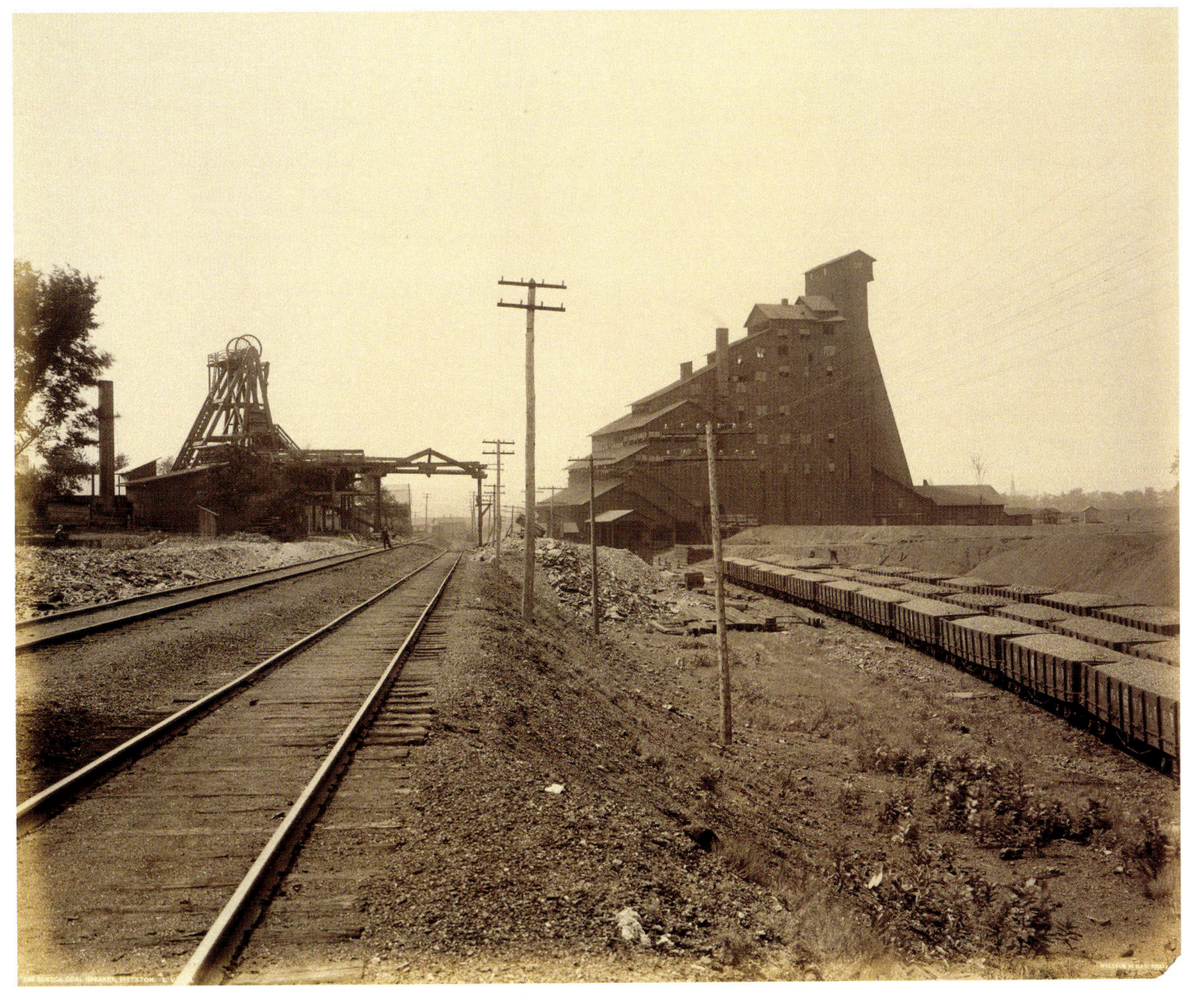

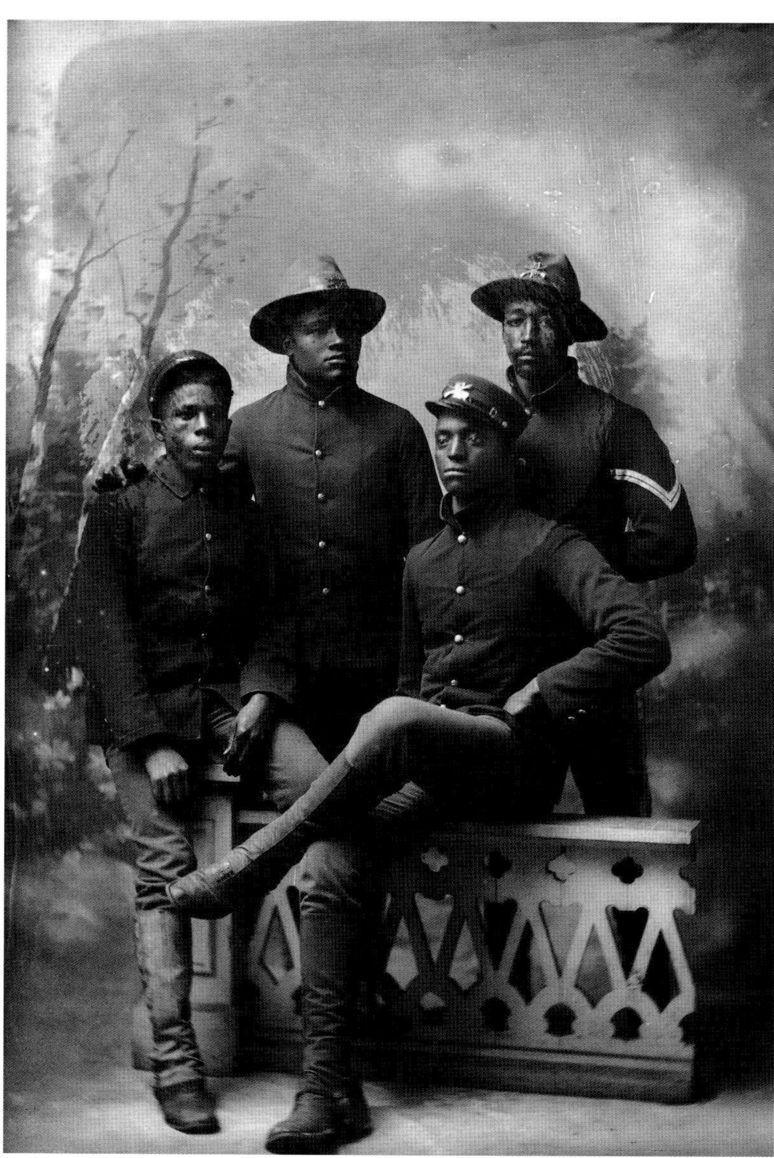

Harrison Putney (1864–1950) or Horace Stevenson (1867–1951)

[Pvt. Paul Schrader of Ottawa, Kansas, and three soldiers of the 23rd Volunteer Infantry], 1899
Gelatin dry plate negative
7 x 5 in. (17.8 x 12.7 cm)
P1978.127.351

Because of Kansas' status as a free state in the pre–Civil War years, the city of Leavenworth's African-American population prospered throughout the nineteenth century. At the time this portrait was made, two photography studios operated by Harrison Putney and Horace Stevenson (both white) openly served the black populace. Sometime in March or April of 1899, Private Paul Schrader (standing on the left) and three other soldiers of the 23rd Kansas Volunteer Infantry visited one of the portrait studios to record their return from the Spanish-American War in Cuba.

After the Civil War, the military offered the most promising job opportunities to African-American males. In 1895, when Cubans revolted against Spanish tyranny, the black American press compared the Cuban fight for independence to the struggle for freedom by southern blacks and called for African-American support. An 1896 Supreme Court decision legitimated "Jim Crow" discrimination, however, and those blacks who tried to volunteer for military duty were rejected. Blacks in Kansas called for the establishment of a "colored" volunteer regiment so they could assist the Cuban effort, while simultaneously proving their loyalty to America. In a political maneuver to gain the black vote in the coming election, Kansas Governor Leedy established the 23rd Volunteer Infantry and quickly sent the unit to Cuba.

Once abroad, the soldiers enthusiastically performed their duties, such as guarding Spanish prisoners of war and restoring services to San Luis Province by repairing bridges, improving roads, and establishing modern sanitary facilities. The 23rd were commended by their superiors, but when they returned from Cuba to Leavenworth, they received no public celebrations in their honor. In a horribly ironic turn, their expression of loyalty through military service actually increased prejudice against them, and lynching was soon on the rise. As these four soldiers paused to record this historic moment for American blacks, the photographer crystallized the complex feelings in their expressions, capturing the pride in their accomplishments coupled with the frustration over the lack of respect due them.

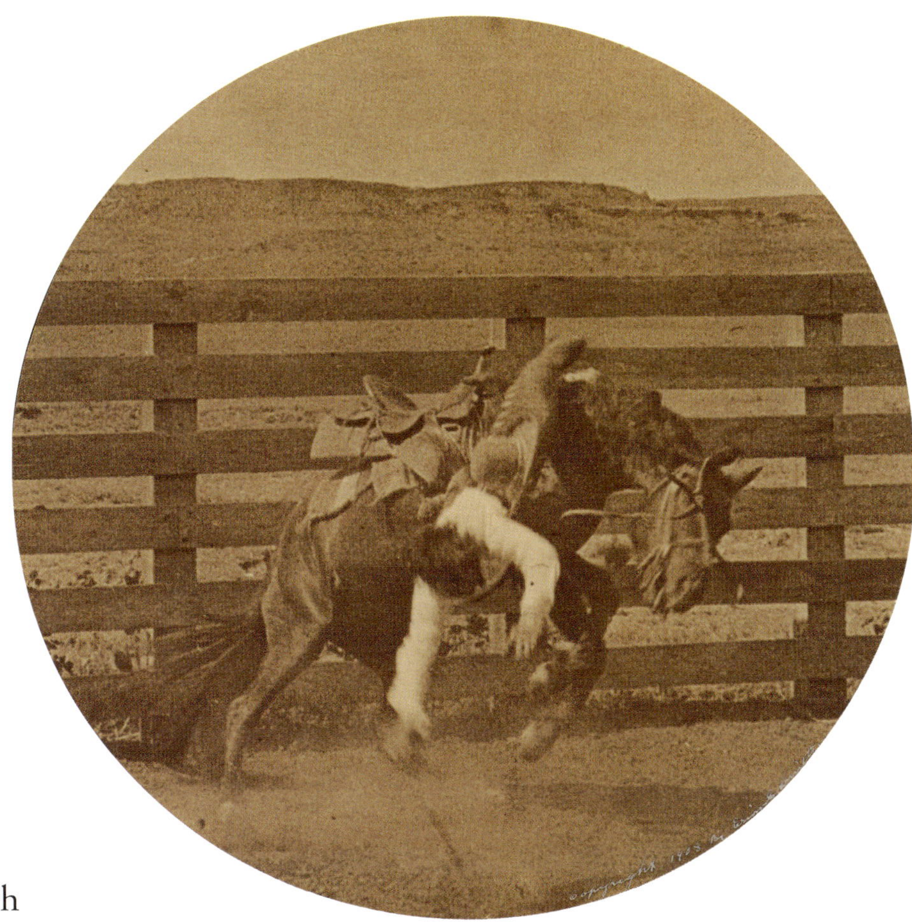

Erwin E. Smith
(1886–1947)

Monclavio Lucero, a Mexican Bronc Buster,
Being Thrown by a Bronc in the LS Corral, LS Ranch, Texas, 1907, print 1936
Gelatin silver print
8 x 17 in. (20.3 x 43.2 cm)
Bequest of Mary Alice Pettis
P1986.42.396

Erwin Evans Smith was driven to document the southwestern cowboy and the culture of the open range before that way of life vanished. Growing up in North Texas, Smith had always wanted to be a cowboy and an artist, believing that through his art he could help preserve a segment of the Old West. While attending art schools in Chicago and Boston, he realized that only a few areas still practiced ranching in the old style and, therefore, spent his summers photographing throughout West Texas and parts of New Mexico and Arizona. Although he originally intended to use his photographs as studies for paintings and sculpture, he eventually learned to appreciate the aesthetic potential of the photographs themselves and produced some of the best-known images of cowboy life.

In 1907, Smith spent over two months—more time than he spent with any other outfit—photographing on the LS Ranch, a spread west of Amarillo and just east of the New Mexican border. There, he produced over 200 images, including some of his best work. Smith wrote to the LS foreman before arriving and questioned him about the outfit's planned activities for the summer, asking specifically if he had "any horses that will pitch and men that will ride them?" When Monclavio Lucero took on the task of breaking one of the wild horses, Smith got into the corral with his hand-held camera and took at least twelve exposures of the unrehearsed and dramatic action. The photographer captured the repeated attempts to get a blanket and saddle on the horse, recording the horse's agile leaps and twists as it tried to unseat the rider. In this climactic shot, Smith selected a circular mat to closely focus the eye on the action.

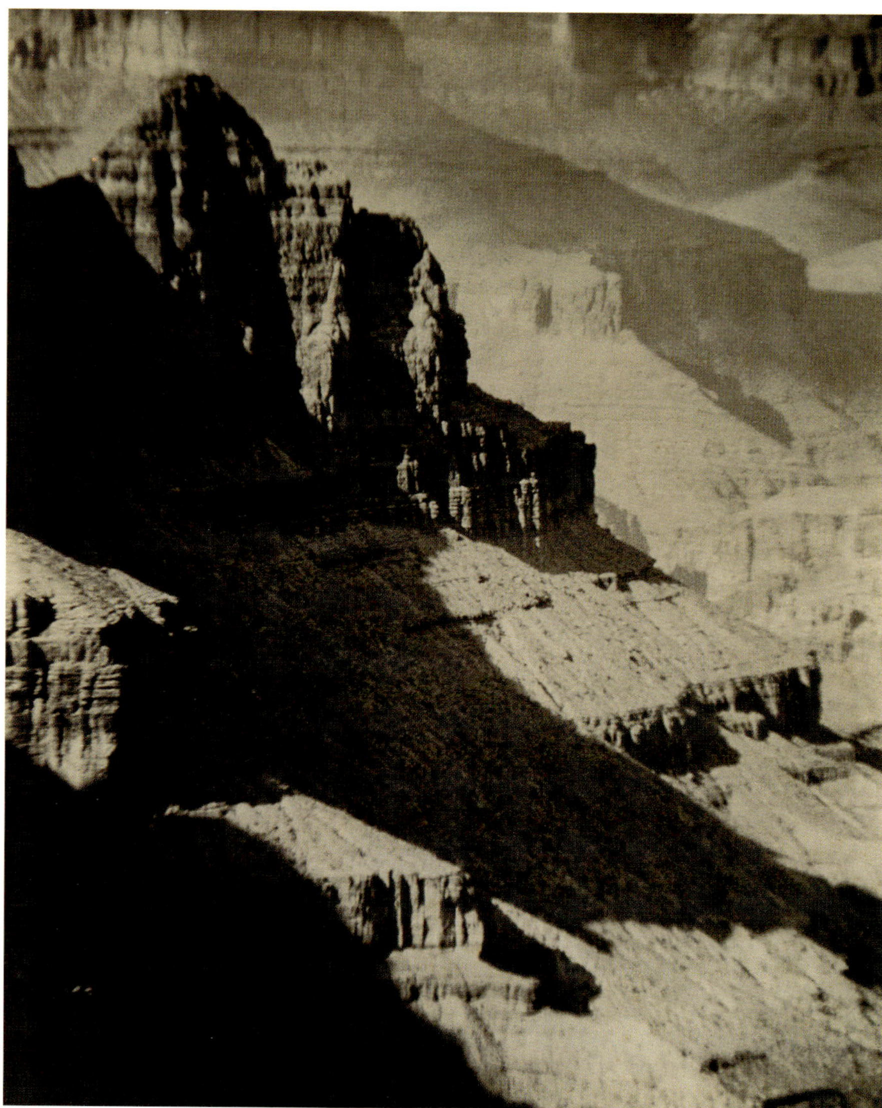

Alvin Langdon Coburn (1882–1966)

The Temple of Ohm, Grand Canyon, 1911, print 1914
Gum platinum print
16 x 12¾ in. (40.6 x 32.4 cm)
Purchase with funds provided by the Council of the Amon Carter Museum
P1996.3

The nineteenth-century explorers who surveyed the Grand Canyon region struggled to describe its wonders. In an attempt to assign meaning to the landscape, they named the major features of the land with conventions that referenced a mythological or religious past. By the end of the century, the canyon had come to represent the consummate beauty of the American continent and the supremacy of the nation. Not until the first railroad line reached the south rim of the Grand Canyon in 1901, however, did the site become a major tourist destination. Recognizing that artists' renderings of the national treasure could promote the area and attract more riders, the Santa Fe Railroad sponsored working trips to the area in return for paintings. Tourism increased so drastically that in 1908 President Roosevelt set aside the area as a national monument to try to stem the tide of tourists.

The damage had already been done, though, and the growing ranks of tourists included modernist artists, attracted by the contours of the land and its suitability to abstraction. Alvin Langdon Coburn was one of the first modernists to depict land formations. As a student of Eastern religions and the occult, he appreciated the religious and mythological references and valued the landscape for its powers of spiritual awakening. "There is a wealth of fine material out here," he wrote to photographer Karl Struss in 1912, "and I feel that I have struck an entirely new note in the things that I have done."

The experience was transforming and led Coburn to create the first known cubist-inspired photographs the following year. In his autobiography he wrote, "It was a day of fast-moving clouds racing before the sun, and casting shadows, alternately concealing and revealing. In a moment all would be changed. . . . Fascinated by the natural views from high altitudes . . . the following year I photographed equally fascinating though quite different man-made views from the top of New York's skyscrapers."

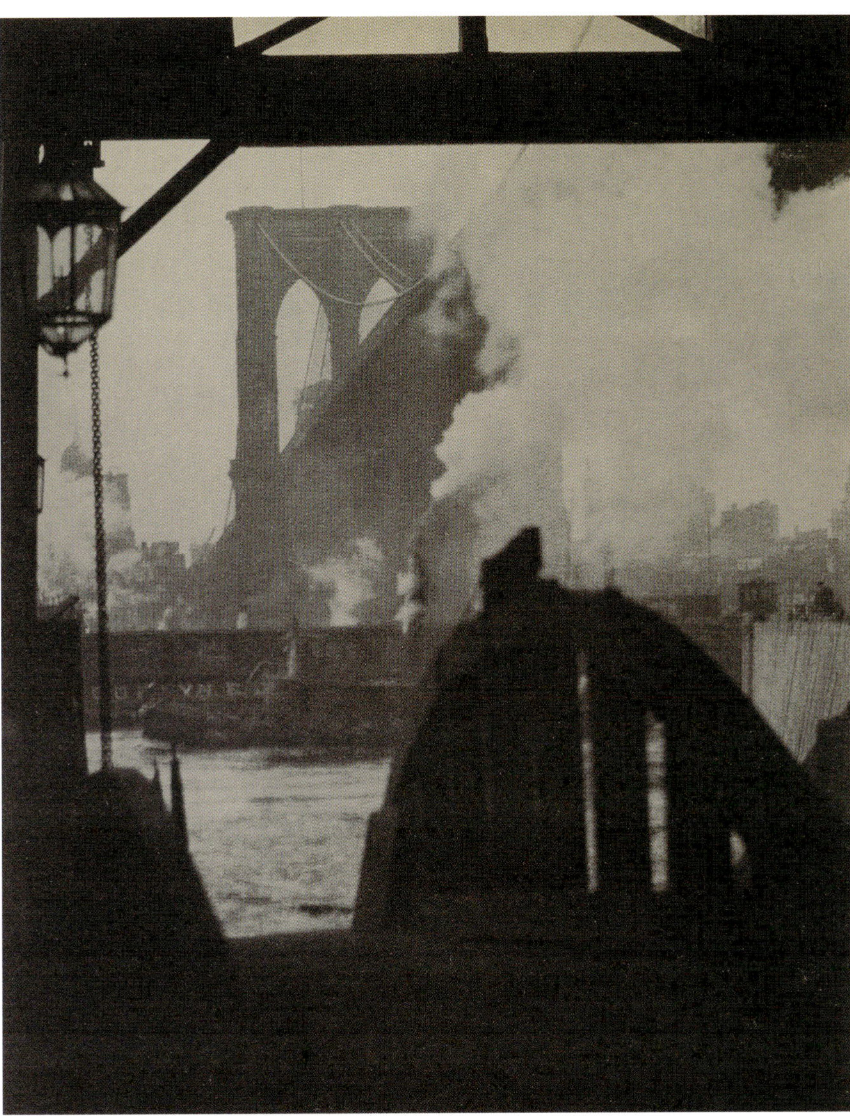

Karl Struss (1886–1981)

Brooklyn Bridge from Ferry Slip. Late Afternoon, 1912
Platinum print
4⅞ x 3¹¹⁄₁₆ in. (12.3 x 9.4 cm)
Copyright 1983, Amon Carter Museum, Fort Worth, Texas
P1983.23.82

When Struss created this view of the Brooklyn Bridge and Manhattan skyline from the Fulton Ferry Terminal on the Brooklyn shore, New York City, the nation's manufacturing, commercial, and financial leader, was experiencing unprecedented economic and physical growth. The bridge played both a real and a symbolic role in this growth, easing transportation between Brooklyn and Manhattan while fueling the imagination of the artists, writers, and tourists who flocked there.

With its Gothic stone towers and steel cables, the Brooklyn Bridge was also an apt symbol for the link between Old World tradition and New World innovation. The structure became a favorite subject for artists, and those returning from study in Europe found it especially well suited to the modern art movement. They utilized compositional tools like fragmentation, overlapping transparencies, and compressed space to depict the bridge as a representation of great forces at work.

Karl Struss was a New Yorker during this exciting time for the city and for art. He was fascinated with the city's dynamism. From 1908 to 1912, he studied photography at Columbia University's Teachers College, where, in addition to learning the soft-focus style of pictorial photography from Clarence White, he also assumed the abstract compositional philosophy of Arthur Wesley Dow. By framing the bridge and skyline scene beneath the ferry slip's piers and using the smoke of the ships to partially hide the bridge, Struss compressed the foreground and background onto a single plane. Just as the Brooklyn Bridge symbolized a link between forces, Struss was the bridge between old and new forms of seeing by combining soft-focus pictorialism with the flattened perspective and space compression of modernism.

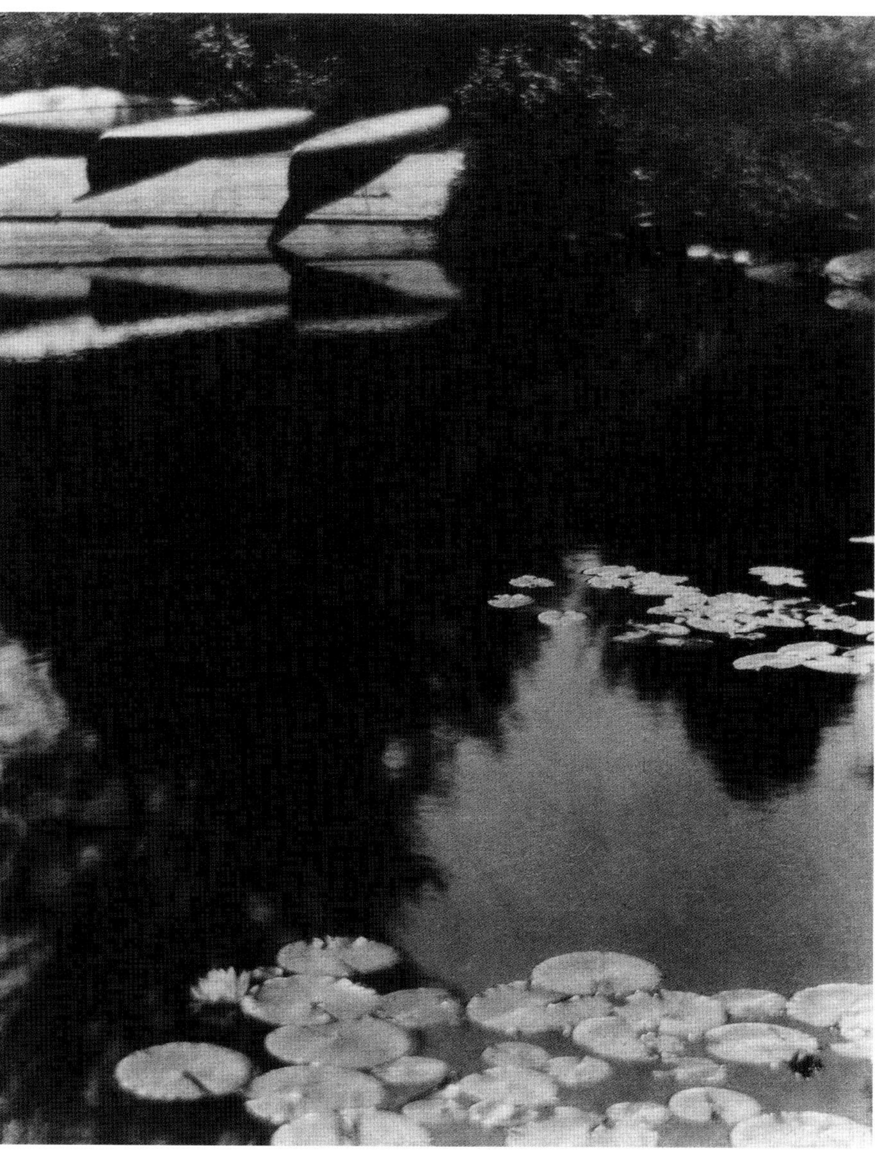

Clara Sipprell
(1885–1975)

Lily Pads and Canoes, Thetford – Vermont, ca. 1919
Platinum print
9 3/16 x 7 3/16 in. (23.3 x 18.3 cm)
P1988.15.2

This unconventional composition of a lily pad-strewn pond with three overturned canoes on the bank reflects the artist's understanding of and comfort with the principles of pictorial design. Although Clara Sipprell was primarily a self-taught photographer, her family's connections with educators in Buffalo placed her in close contact with the most progressive education philosophy in the country. After moving to New York City at the age of thirty, Sipprell met the leaders of the education community there, including Arthur Wesley Dow, head of the art department at Columbia University's Teachers College. Dow—whose widely read book *Composition: A Series of Exercises in Art Structure for the Use of Students and Teachers* (1899) disseminated the Japanese concept of composition—was so impressed with Sipprell's understanding of this concept that he let her use his studio.

Clara Sipprell made this view on the grounds of Hanoum, a summer camp for girls in Thetford, Vermont. The owners, Charles and Charlotte Farnsworth, had known Sipprell in Buffalo. They started the camp in 1909 at the request of students at Horace Mann High School, which was connected to Columbia University, to provide athletic education for young girls and prepare them for life's demanding roles. They took the name Hanoum from the Turkish word for lady, inspired by Charles Farnsworth's mother who had been a missionary there. The couple asked Sipprell to produce images for a recruitment brochure in 1917. After continuing to visit and photograph in Thetford for several summers, Sipprell eventually set up a seasonal studio there, which she kept into the 1930s.

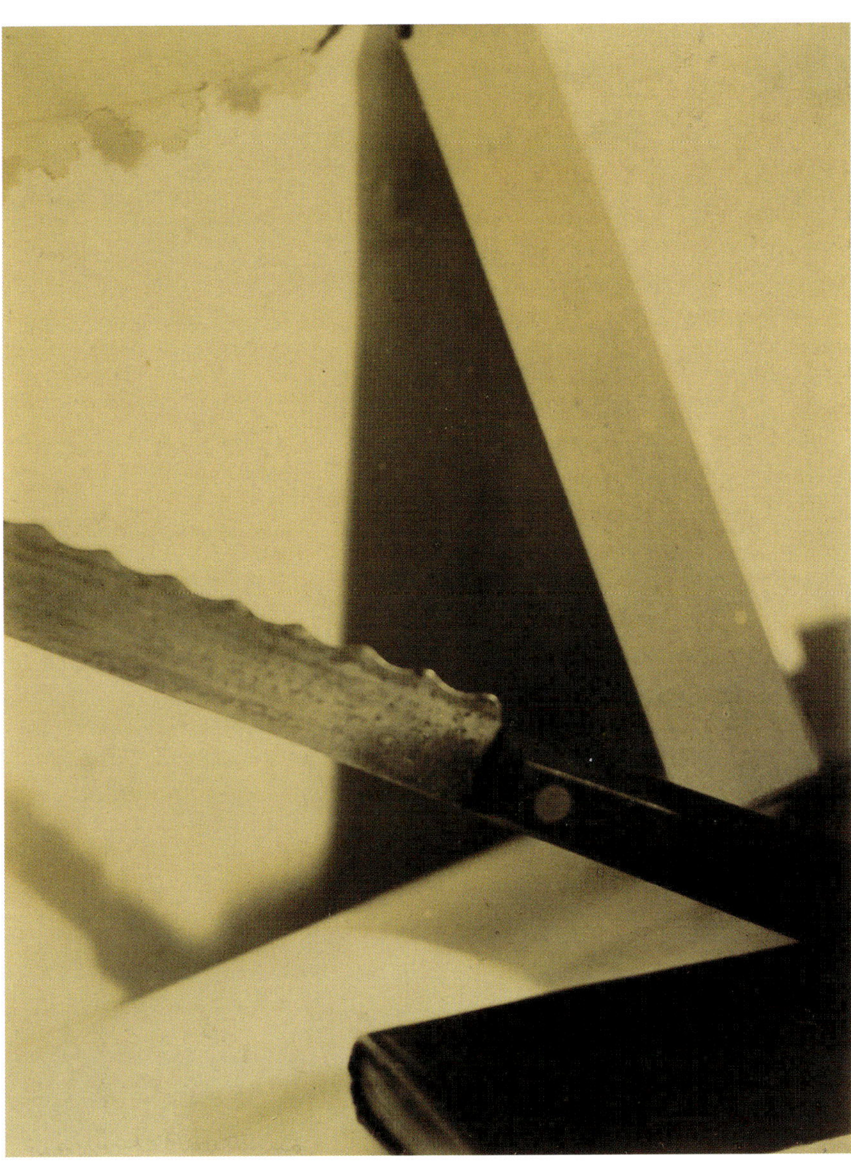

Margaret Watkins (1884–1969)

Design-Angles, 1919
Gaslight (chloride) print
8⅛ x 6⅛ in. (20.6 x 15.5 cm)
P1983.41.3

Watkins created this abstract still life both as an exercise in composition and design and as an example for her students at the Clarence White School of Photography. She began taking classes at the school in 1914, and by 1917 she was so accomplished that White asked her to join the faculty. A list of composition problems she proposed for a summer school class included "an angular still life" and "a curved still life." She instructed her students to use such specific subjects as "white towels, two books, spoons, and glasses of milk or water." Watkins learned these design-problem techniques from the classes she took at the school, which included lectures by the avant-garde painter Max Weber. Weber emphasized the importance of two-dimensional design in photography, encouraging his listeners to reorganize the forms and fill the frame. The school also instructed the students—who were mostly women—to make a profession of photography and recommended advertising as an appropriate career. Watkins was one of the first to show such potential.

Watkins' innovative still lifes, created in her Greenwich Village kitchen with common utensils, were criticized for their unconventional subject matter. Basing art on such mundane objects went against the grain of the more conservative pictorialist style, which treated subjects nobly. Watkins countered the attack in an article titled "Advertising and Photography," which she wrote for a 1926 issue of *Pictorial Photography in America*. She explained that modernist art philosophies were influencing advertising to give greater priority to design: "With Cézanne, Matisse, and Picasso, came a new approach . . . beauty of subject was superceded by beauty of design . . . . Even the plain businessman, suspicious of 'art stuff,' perceives that his product is enhanced by fine tone-spacing and the beauty of contrasted textures. And the purchaser, however indifferent to circular rhythms, unconsciously responds to the clarity of statement achieved by stressing the essential form of the article."

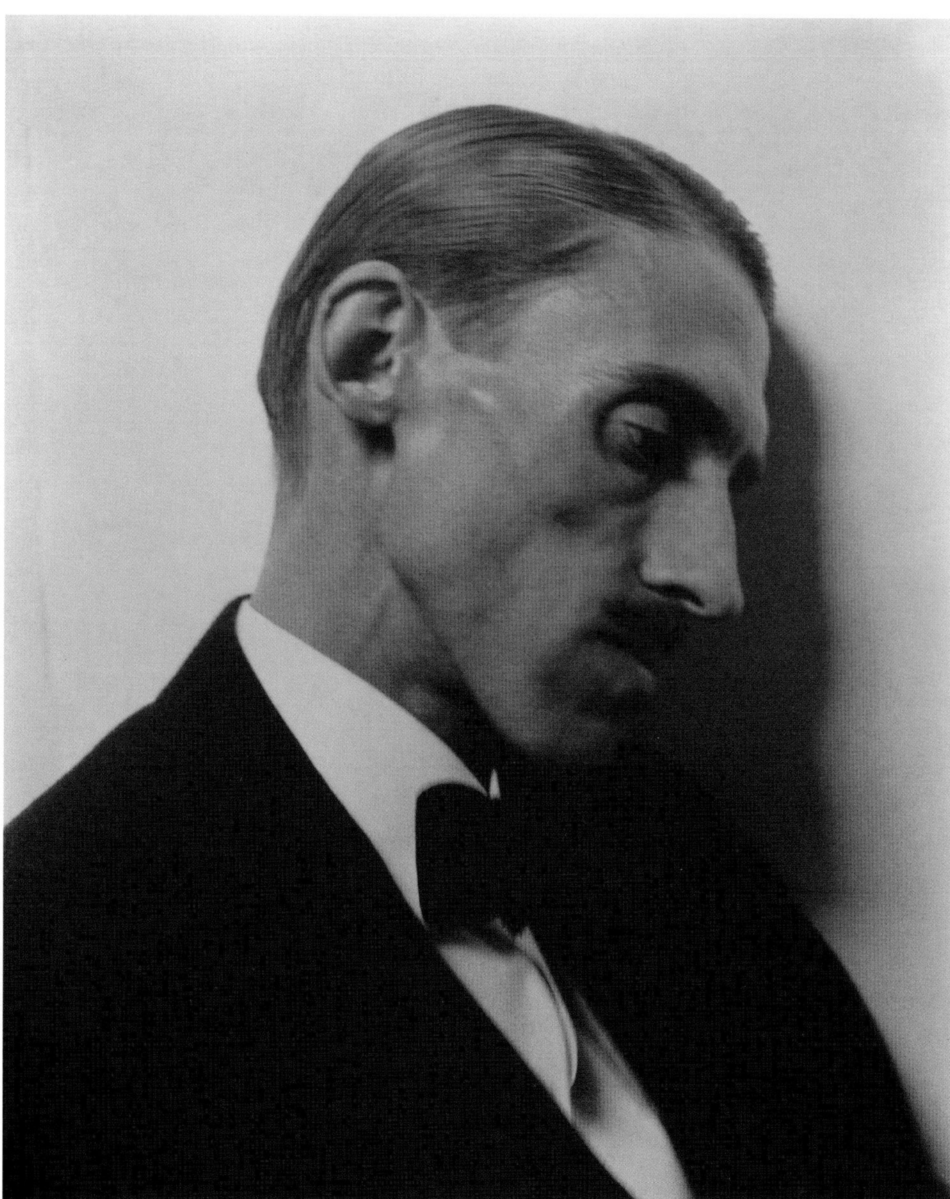

Alfred Stieglitz
(1864–1946)

Charles Demuth, 1923
Gelatin silver print
$9\frac{1}{2}$ x $7\frac{5}{8}$ in. (24.1 x 19.4 cm)
Gift of Doris Bry

P1998.75

Alfred Stieglitz's significance to the history of photography is unparalleled. He led the effort to proclaim the artistic potential of the medium in the late-nineteenth century and the early decades of the twentieth century in three significant ways: through his editorship of the art journals *Camera Notes* and *Camera Work*, by his management of a series of influential New York City galleries, and with his own photography. In that endeavor, he met and became friends with many of the leading artists and avant-garde writers of the day. When these people visited his exhibition rooms, he often made a point of photographing them.

When Stieglitz created this compelling portrait, Charles Demuth was a well-known watercolorist and artistic bon vivant who had innovatively begun to adapt the flattened planes of cubism to vernacular American architecture. Although he was in the second year of a draining treatment for diabetes, Demuth was on the verge of becoming one of this country's most important modernist painters. Stieglitz's image sensitively captures both Demuth's dandy-like personality and the exhaustion brought on by his intense diet and insulin regimen. Upon seeing it, Demuth wrote poignantly to the photographer, "You have me in a fix. Shall I remain ill retaining the look, die, considering 'that moment' the climax of my 'looks,' or live and change. I think the head is one of the most beautiful things that I have ever known in the world of art."

A significant example of the important artworks that Stieglitz originally gave to his wife, Georgia O'Keeffe, this photograph is part of the Amon Carter Museum's outstanding collection of Stieglitz Circle works by such artists as O'Keeffe, Demuth, Marsden Hartley, Arthur Dove, John Marin, Paul Strand, and Edward Steichen.

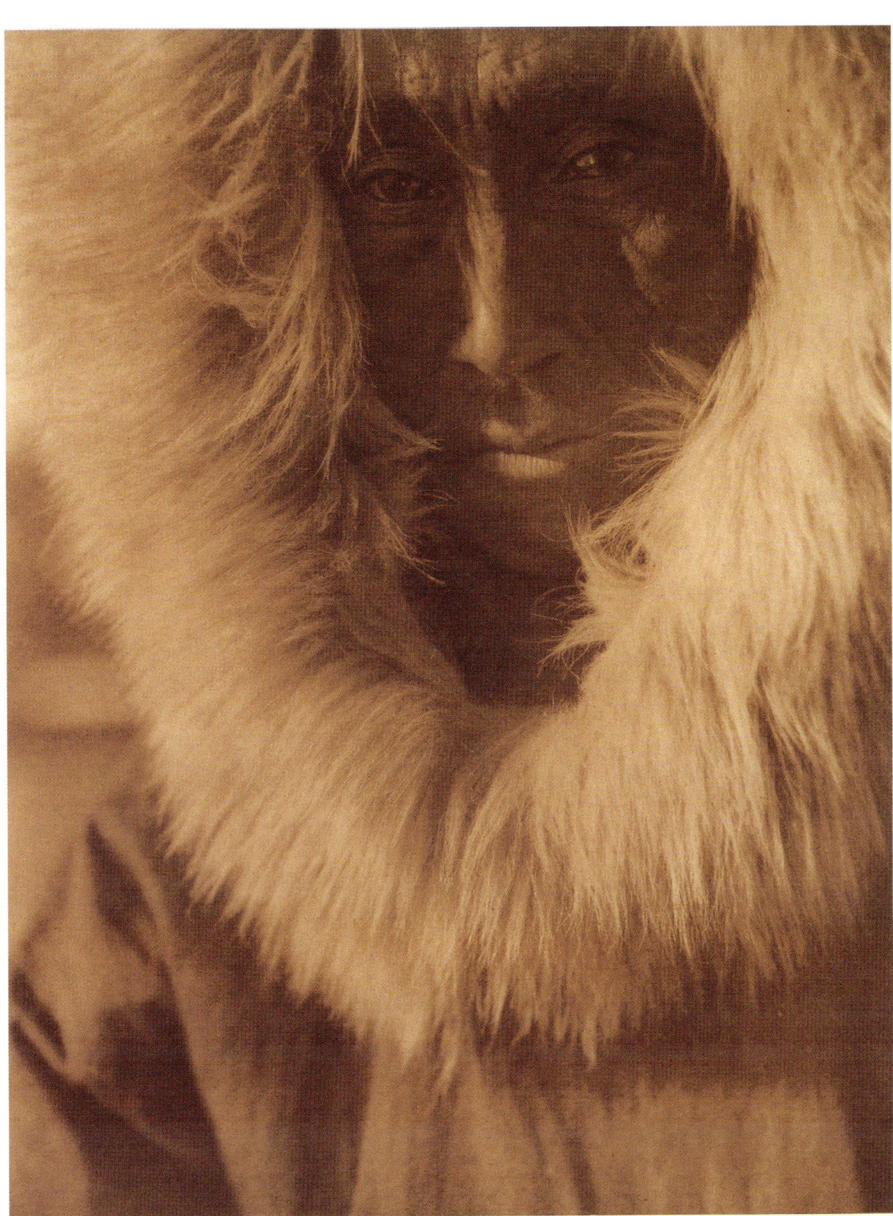

Edward S. Curtis
(1868–1952)

Jájuk-Selawik, 1927
Photogravure on tissue
13 x 16½ in. (33 x 41.9 cm)
P1977.1.720

By 1927 Edward Curtis and his assistants had photographed every major indigenous tribe west of the Mississippi. That June, to complete the final section of his impressive multi-volume portrait of North America's Indian cultures, they sailed north from Nome, determined to record the Inuit communities located within the Arctic Circle. The trip to Alaska marked the closing of a circle for Curtis. Twenty-eight years earlier he had made his first visit to the region as chief photographer for Edward H. Harriman's geographical survey of the Alaskan coast.

Undaunted by increasingly difficult weather and local missionaries who actively opposed his project, Curtis reached the Selawik River that September and successfully photographed members of the Inupiat tribe. This remarkable portrait is one of the strongest photographs of the session. The subject's hood dominates the image, delivering a tactile lushness in contrast to the image's shallow depth of field. Yet the man's piercing gaze establishes the portrait's true power.

Rough seas, blizzards, and tremendous winds beset Curtis' leaking, flat-bottomed boat as he and his crew started their return south. Yet the photographer insisted on stopping at Wales, along the Bering Strait, to make a few more photographs before heading for safety. When they finally arrived at Nome, belying reports of their demise, every inhabitant of the amazed town turned out to welcome them.

Curtis published this portrait in the twentieth and final volume of *The North American Indian*. Having taken thirty years to complete, the project combined an extensive ethnological text with over 2,000 plates drawn from some 40,000 images. Documenting more than eighty North American tribes, it gave a face to the indigenous peoples of the American continent at a point when Anglo culture was overtaking them. This image comes from the Amon Carter Museum's nearly complete set of large, sepia-toned photogravure plates that accompanied the volumes.

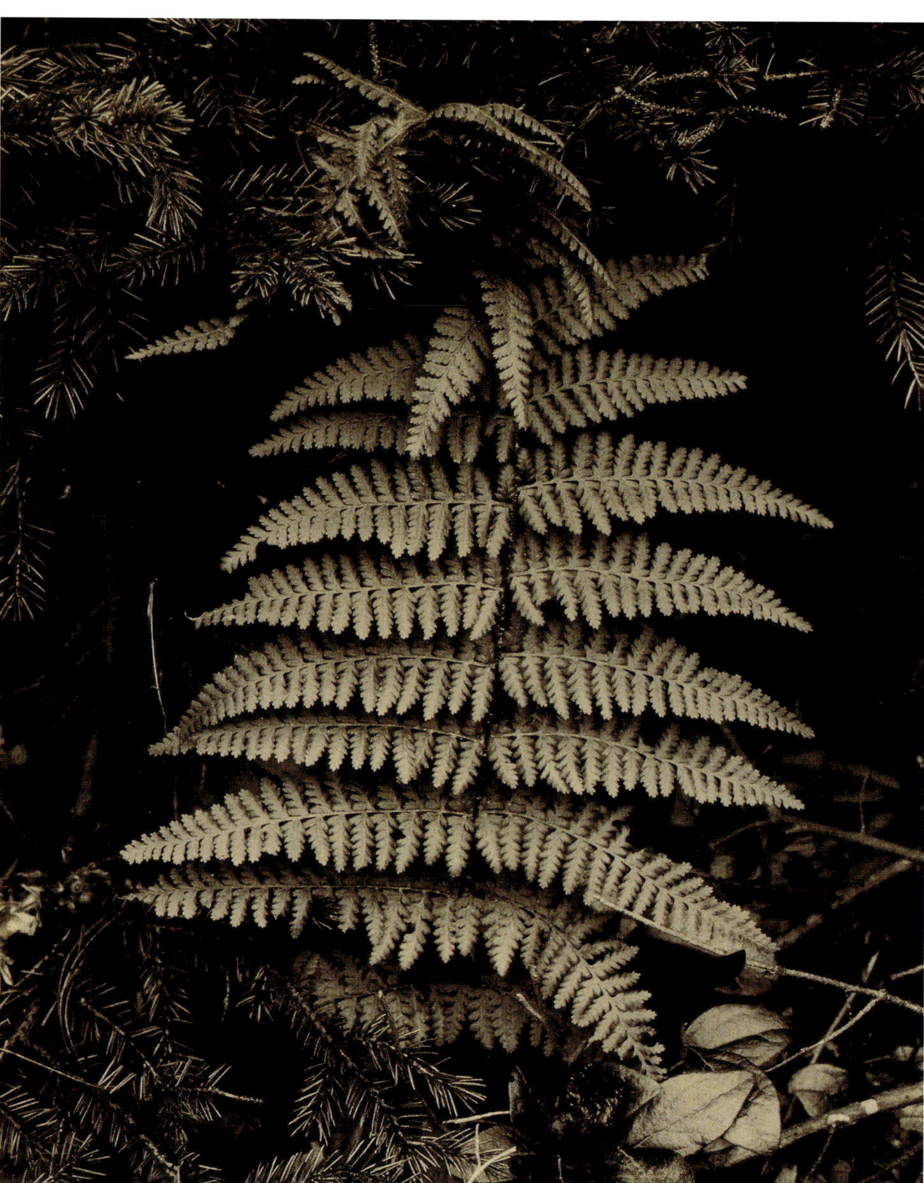

Paul Strand (1890–1976)

Fern, New England, 1928
Platinum print
10 x 8 in. (25.4 x 20.3 cm)

P1995.8

Paul Strand gained renown in the 1910s as the first photographer to successfully capture on film the look and feel of modern, urban America. His photographs of the streets, alleys, and people of New York have a gritty realism, often bound within a closely cropped network of flattened, cubist-inspired space. While he remained ambivalent about modern industrial commerce, he appreciated the attention to craft that at times poked through consumer culture and, in the early 1920s, drew attention to the fine handiwork inscribing his movie camera by making close-up photographs of both the camera and the equipment used to make it.

By the late 1920s, however, Strand, like many of his colleagues, had stopped believing in the possibilities of urban reform. While some of his associates, like Waldo Frank, Marsden Hartley, and John Marin, turned to rural and indigenous America for answers, he decided to lovingly delineate the details of nature. This tapestry-like portrait of a fern frond is one of the most elegant examples of that work. The image exudes texture and the dark, quiet mystery of New England woods. Here is a fine specimen of nature's craftsmanship elaborated in the unparalleled tonal nuances available only in platinum printing.

In 1929 the master photographer Alfred Stieglitz showed Strand's nature studies, including this image, in his Intimate Gallery to broad critical acclaim. The sculptor Gaston Lachaise wrote a glowing exhibition introduction, but theater director Harold Clurman provided the most astute critique of the photographer's new work. Drawing attention to what he called the "splendid isolation" of Strand's plants, Clurman wrote the following in his review of the exhibition for the October 1929 issue of *Creative Art*: "They do not come forward to speak in any voice but their own, they do not permit us to approach them with any sentimental concern, any benign interpretation."

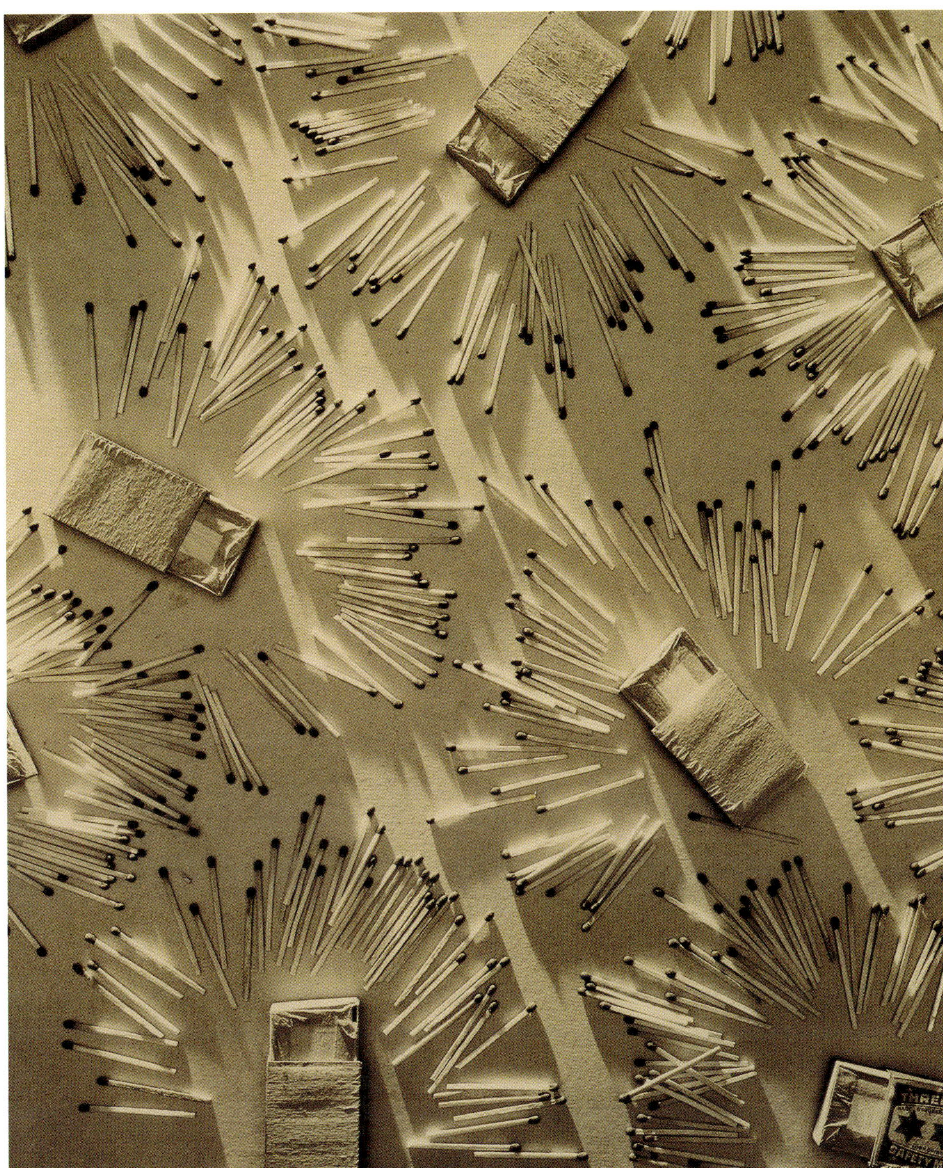

Edward Steichen (1879–1973)

Stehli Silk Design, 1926
Gelatin silver print
9⁹⁄₁₆ x 7⅝ in. (24.1 x 19.4 cm)
Permission of Joanna T. Steichen
Purchase with funds provided by the Council of the Amon Carter Museum
P1998.48

While Paul Strand drew an absolute line between art and commerce, Edward Steichen freely and proudly mixed the two. Where Strand asserted that commercial demands corrupted artistic independence, Steichen retorted that whether a photograph presented a celebrity portrait, commercial shot, or documentary view, its intended function remained far less important than whether it captured a viewer's eye and emotions. His photograph *Stehli Silk Design* offers a supreme example of that philosophy.

Steichen was a hugely popular commercial photographer when he created this image. He regularly produced elegant fashion studies and portraits of celebrities for Condé Nast and was able to command top prices for his services. That renown, combined with the photographer's reputation for experimentation, is surely what drew the Stehli Silk art director, Ruzzie Green, to approach him in 1926 to create images that could be transformed into innovative dress fabrics. Upon gaining Green's agreement that he could use whatever props he desired, Steichen set to work photographing patterns of thread, spectacles, sugar, carpet tacks, and even mothballs. This photograph's array of stick matches splayed between their overturned boxes is one of the strongest images to come out of the assignment. Appearing to extend indefinitely in all directions, the print projects a vivid texture and luminous light that seem to grow directly out of the paper. Not surprisingly, Stehli Silk transformed this image into an orange silk weave that carried a vibrant, shimmering grace.

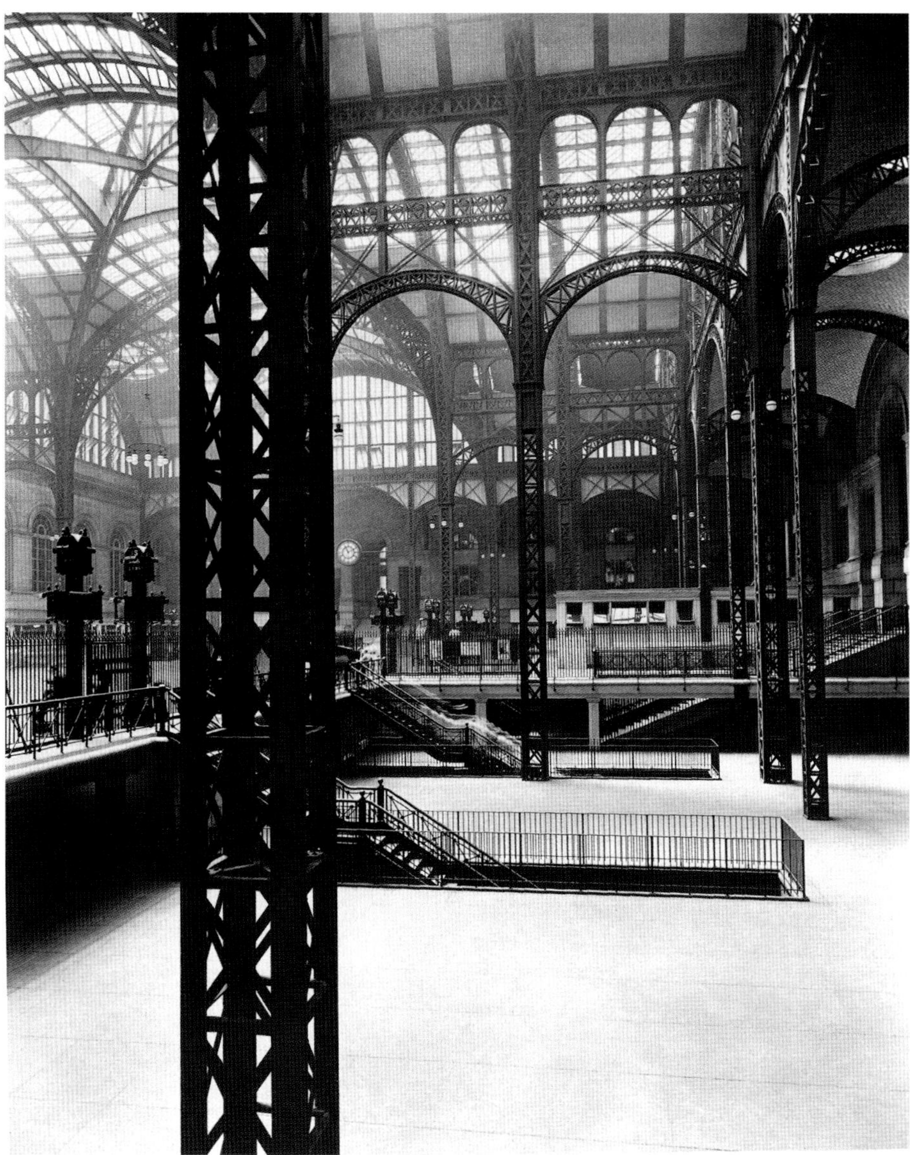

Berenice Abbott
(1898–1991)

Pennsylvania Station Interior, 1936,
print 1979
Gelatin silver print
$9^{3}/_{8}$ x $7^{9}/_{16}$ in. (23.9 x 19.1 cm)

P1980.36

A decade before Abbott made this interior view of New York's Pennsylvania Station, she was living in Paris and met the photographer Eugène Atget, who had been photographing that city's streets and architecture for thirty years. Inspired by his dedication and hauntingly beautiful photographs, Abbott was determined to do the same with New York City when she returned to America in 1929. At first she worked independently to complete the monumental *Changing New York* project, but from 1935 through 1939 she finally received support from the Works Progress Administration's Federal Art Project. The ambitious undertaking produced over 300 images from more than 700 negatives. The negative for this image, although not included in *Changing New York*, was discovered later and became one of her best-known images.

After photographing the Greyhound Bus Terminal on July 14, 1936, Abbott moved across the street to photograph Pennsylvania Station. Designed by McKim, Mead, and White and completed in 1911, the railroad station covered the two city blocks bordered by 31st and 33rd Streets and 7th and 8th Avenues.

Abbott concentrated on the utilitarian design of the glass-roofed concourse with its steel structural supports. The concourse accessed the subway tracks below, yet the glass roof provided so much natural light that artificial light was not required during the day.

Photographing early in the morning when the space was nearly empty, Abbott used a very slow shutter speed, reducing movement to a vague blur. The steel girder's bold line in the foreground contrasts with the soft, filtered light coming from the glass ceiling and the fluid line of figures descending the steps, providing an apt metaphor for the contrast of old and new in changing New York. Pennsylvania Station was demolished in 1965, resulting in a public outcry and leading to the establishment of the Landmarks Preservation Commission to protect historic buildings.

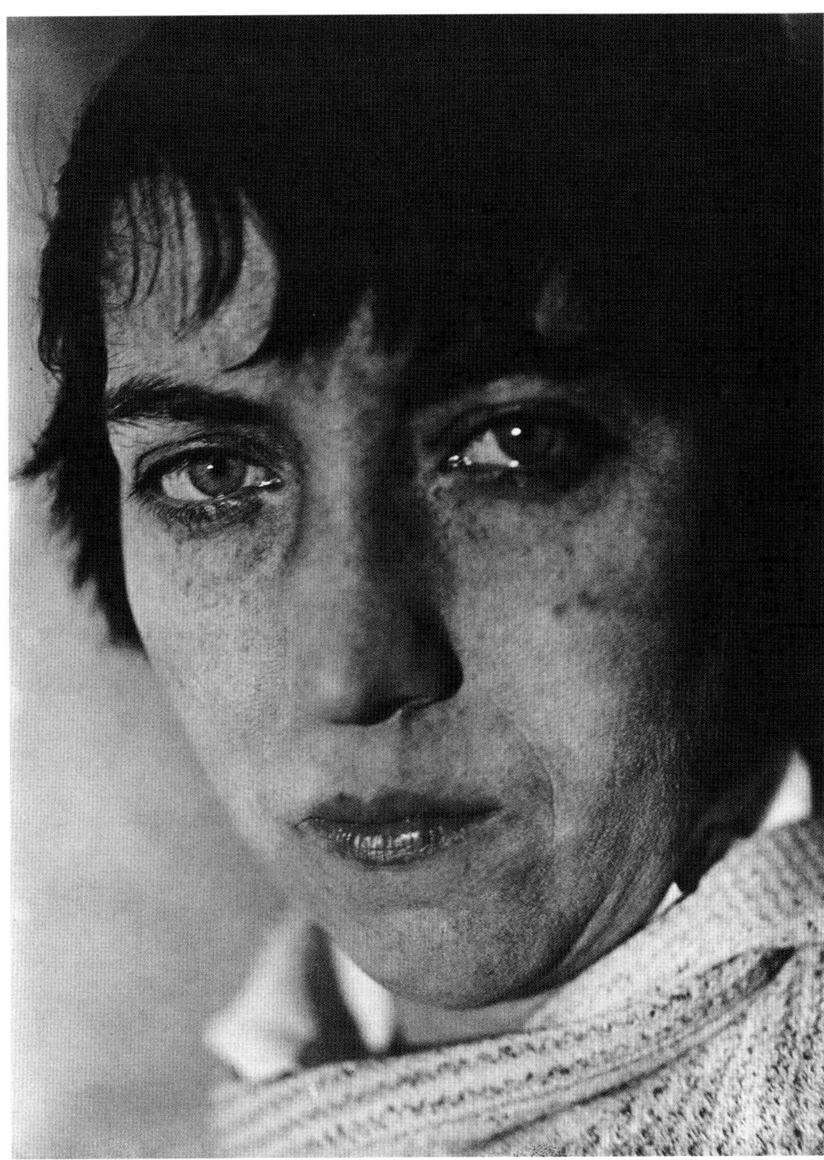

Walker Evans
(1903–1975)

Berenice Abbott, ca. 1930
Gelatin silver print
6½ x 4¹¹⁄₁₆ in. (16.5 x 11.9 cm)
© Walker Evans Archives,
The Metropolitan Museum of Art
P1978.17.1

Walker Evans had only recently met Berenice Abbott when he made this piercing study. She had moved to New York in 1929 after living in Paris most of the decade. There, she had worked as an assistant to the artist Man Ray and was a popular portrait photographer of artists and writers. She rescued Eugène Atget's negatives after his death, brought them to New York, and was in the process of printing them. Abbott and Evans were moved by Atget's style of objective documentation and studied his aesthetic in order to apply it to New York City. Evans' photographs of the Brooklyn Bridge had just been published with Hart Crane's poem *The Bridge*. He acquired two view cameras, and Abbott coached him and let him use her darkroom facilities.

Although the two photographers were concentrating on New York's architecture at this time, both also had experience with portraiture. Abbott did portraits in Paris, and Evans had experimented with self-portraiture by photographing his own shadow and, more recently, using the new photomat machines.

This portrait may have resulted from Abbott demonstrating to Evans how a view camera would affect a close-up portrait. Many people commented on Abbott's eyes: Evans called them "woozy" while the writer Lincoln Kirstein referred to them as "kewpie eyes." By focusing sharply on Abbott's right eye—so much so that much of the rest of the face blurs—Evans draws attention to the intensity with which she viewed all of her subjects, whether city streets, the human face, or the lens of a colleague's camera.

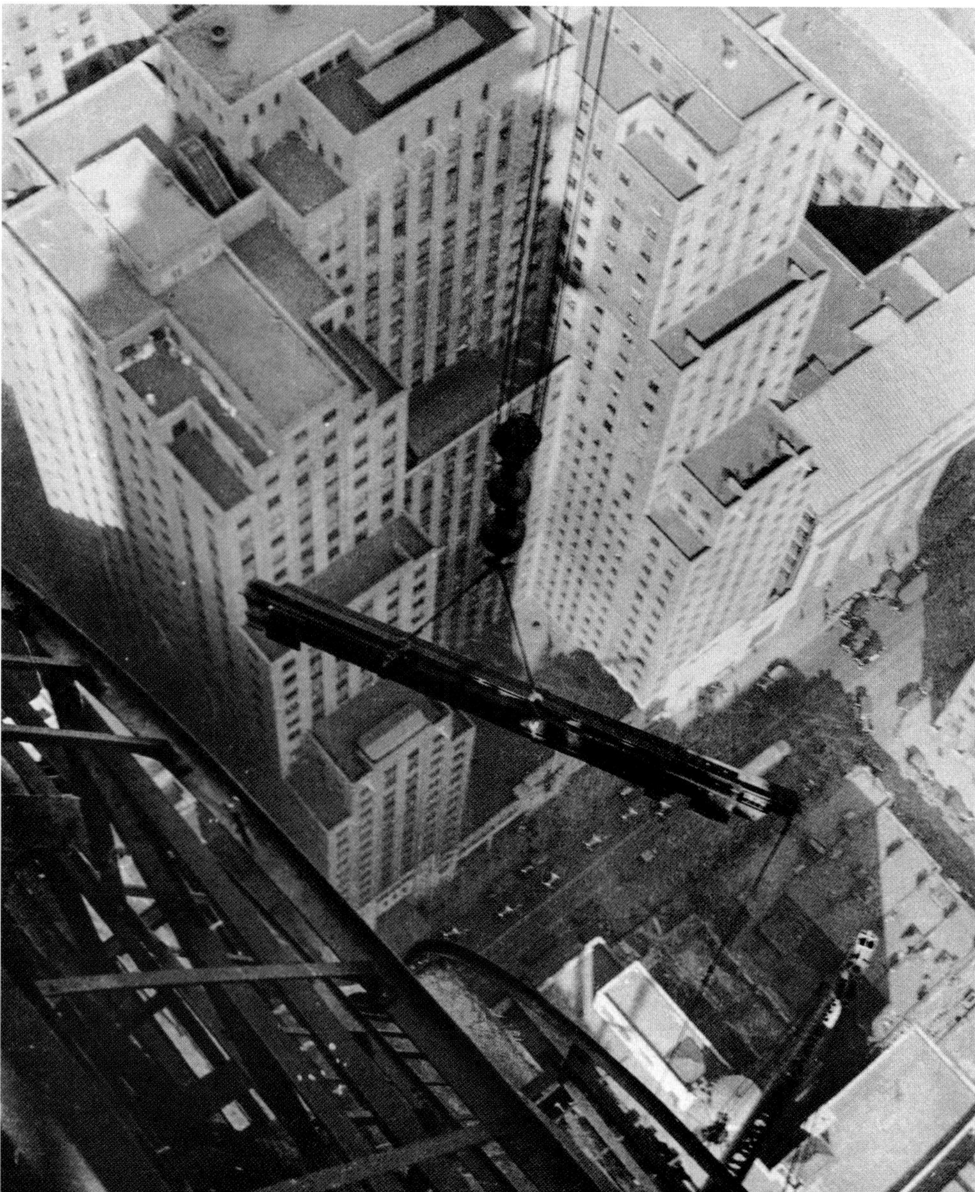

Charles Rivers
(1904–1993)
Shadow of the Chrysler over the Graybar Building while a Load of Steel is Being Relayed from Derrick to Derrick to Reach the Floor Where it is to be Erected into Place, 1929
Gelatin silver print
19½ x 15 13/16 in. (49.5 x 40.2 cm)

P1986.24.1

While helping build New York City's famous Chrysler Building in 1929 and the Empire State Building a year later, Charles Rivers literally created a worker's eye view of the construction activity. With a camera kept in his toolbox, he surreptitiously documented each project from derrick level, photographing both the steel beams that rose high over Manhattan's streets and his fellow workers as they ate lunch.

Rather than heroize the construction activity like his more famous associate, Lewis Hine, Rivers offers an iron-worker's perspective. Where Hine went out of his way to create dizzying views of workers at the edge of space, Rivers evokes the balance necessary for working at such heights. Even this photograph of beams being lifted up to the top recesses of the Chrysler building presents a vision of steady equilibrium. While one clearly sees the cars hundreds of feet below, the stepped roofs of the surrounding buildings offer a Mondrian-like pattern that comfortably carries one's eye up to the weave of already secured beams. Rather than emphasizing the Chrysler's sky-piercing height, the image suggests that Rivers and his fellow workers are filling in the gaps in Manhattan's thick tangle of real estate.

Rivers had been inspired by Hine's earlier photographs of working people, but the two artists' paths never crossed. Although both men photographed the construction of the Empire State Building, Rivers did not realize that Hine had photographed the site until years later. Both men also worked actively for social reform. When the depression brought New York construction to a standstill in the 1930s, Rivers involved himself in movements to create social security, unemployment insurance, and housing for workers.

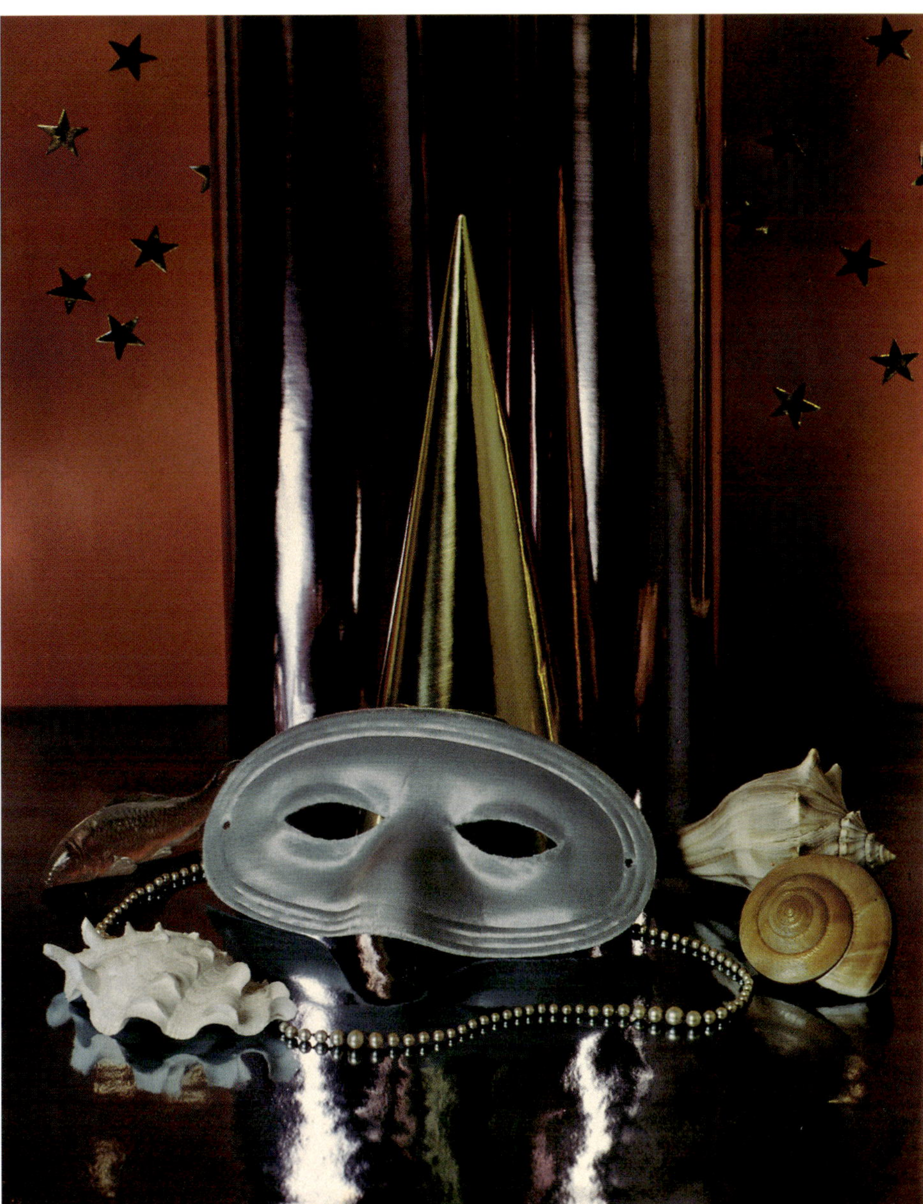

Paul Outerbridge Jr. (1896–1958)

Party Mask with Shells, 1936
Tricolor carbro print
15 1/8 x 10 7/8 in. (38.4 x 27.6 cm)

Courtesy of G. Ray Hawkins
P1996.17

Paul Outerbridge Jr. was unsurpassed as a designer with a camera. In the early 1920s he gained the respect of his peers by redefining advertising photography, integrating a modernist compositional structure of flattened planes into standard product illustrations. In the 1930s he became one of the first photographers to start working in color, taking up the recently perfected tricolor carbro process. A meticulously prepared "sandwich" of delicate cyan, magenta, and yellow tissues, carbro prints became the preferred color medium of the 1930s because they provided lush, unusually nuanced colors of exceptional brilliance and permanence.

This work represents one of Outerbridge's most compelling and important color works. Ostensibly presenting the accoutrements of a costume ball, the photograph is a virtuoso composition of seductive color, texture, and reflection. It both heralds and subverts the factual realism of color in that the image hues are true, but the mask, pearls, and shells float within a liquid space of shimmering reflected light. The effect is otherworldly.

In 1940, Outerbridge took advantage of his reputation as a leading color photographer by publishing the seminal book *Photographing in Color*, wherein he explained his ideas and techniques. But the market for his preoccupation with leisure, beauty, and fantasy was being replaced by the commercial world's new embrace of a colder documentary aesthetic. As his work fell out of favor, he moved to Hollywood in 1943 to satisfy his longtime interest in film. Unable to break into the studio system, he relied on occasional fashion and portrait commissions, supplemented by magazine articles, until his death in 1958.

A meticulous worker, Outerbridge rarely made more than one or two prints of a given image and left behind a core of only about 100 photographs. This masterpiece came from the artist's personal collection and was the first tricolor carbro print to enter the Amon Carter Museum's collection.

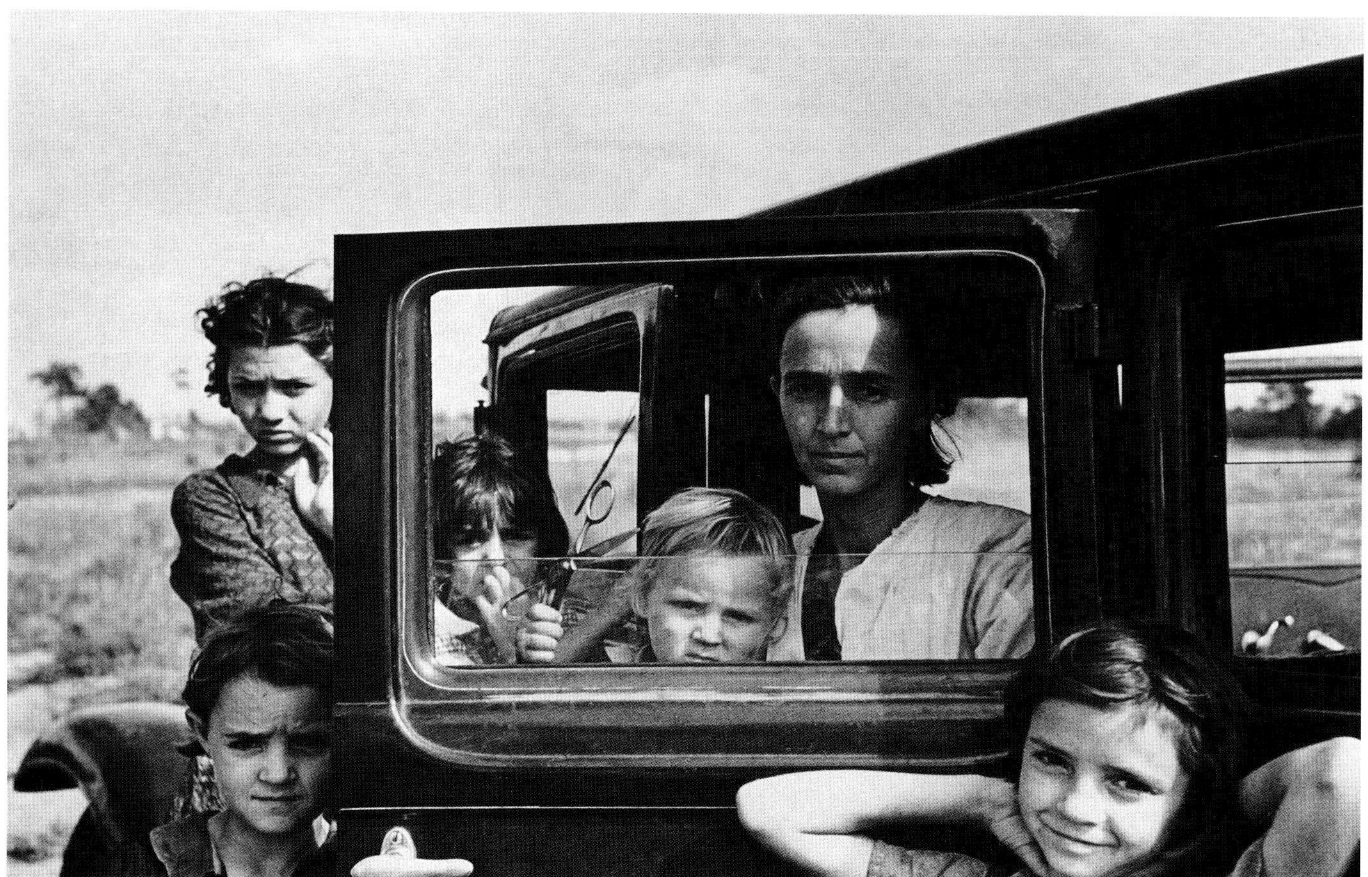

Arthur Rothstein (1915–1985)

Migrant Family, Oklahoma, 1936, print 1981
Gelatin silver print
$8\frac{1}{16}$ x $12\frac{1}{8}$ in. (20.5 x 30.8 cm)

P1998.76.10

In 1935, Roy Stryker, the director of the newly formed Historical Section of the Resettlement Administration (RA), sent Arthur Rothstein into America's heartland to photograph agricultural subjects and the effects of the depression on the people. At the same time, several years of drought culminated in massive dust storms that stripped the land of its soil and caused ruined farmers to lose their land. Government programs encouraged uprooted farmers to migrate in search of better soil. Although Oklahoma, the most adversely affected state, lost many of its residents, the majority stayed, expecting that the rains would eventually return. Others who migrated to California or Oregon missed their homes so much that they moved back, relying on faith and hope.

Rothstein had met Stryker the previous year when he took a course from him at Columbia University and had helped him assemble photographs for a pictorial history of American agriculture. When Stryker joined the RA, he remembered the bright student and hired him to set up the photo lab and order equipment for the New Deal program. Rothstein learned aesthetics from other photographers hired by Stryker, especially Walker Evans and Ben Shahn. He also developed his own portraiture philosophy, keeping the camera below eye level and waiting for a fleeting expression, like a tilt of the head or a twinkle in the eyes.

In order to symbolize this family's migrant lifestyle, Rothstein utilized the car door's window as his primary compositional device. But the animated smile of the girl in the right foreground is what makes the image come alive. While the furrowed brows of the mother and the four children on the left communicate the hardships they endured and their persistent worries for the future, the young girl's almost carefree smile represents persistent optimism in the face of great struggle.

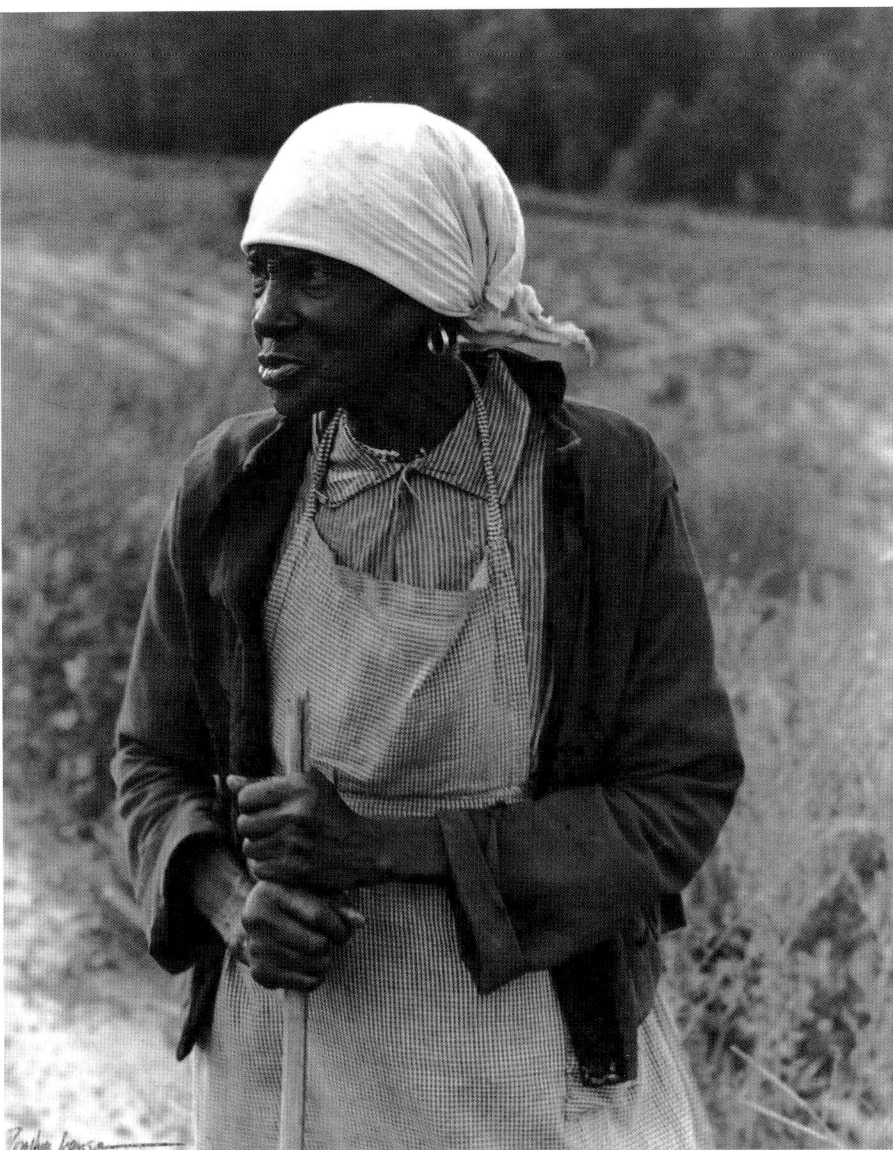

Dorothea Lange
(1895–1965)
Ex-Slave with a Long Memory. Alabama, 1938, print before 1965
Gelatin silver print
$13^{3/8}$ x $10^{3/8}$ in. (33.9 x 26.3 cm)

Gift of Paul S. Taylor
P1965.172.20

When Dorothea Lange photographed this woman, she combined her growing concern for the plight of the American poor with years of experience as a portrait photographer. In the mid-1910s, she had apprenticed in Arnold Genthe's fashionable New York City portrait studio and then ran her own studio in San Francisco, where she catered to society's elite. Following the stock market crash in 1929, her portrait business slackened. She began to focus on street photography, documenting labor strikes and the city's homeless population. In 1935 she met and began a long collaboration with Paul Taylor, an economics professor at the University of California at Berkeley, who soon became her husband and a moral guide directing her work. Taylor, a nationally known scholar of agricultural economics and labor, advocated the social benefits of land ownership and believed that migrant labor and farm tenancy were crippling the American economy. Taylor and Lange's documentation of the situation resulted in the 1939 publication of *An American Exodus: A Record of Human Erosion.*

Throughout the 1930s, Lange produced documentary photographs for several government agencies. She started with an assignment to study the growing numbers of dust bowl refugees migrating to California and eventually worked with Roy Stryker for the Resettlement Administration (RA)—renamed the Farm Security Administration in 1937. Stryker's goal with the RA's photodocumentation was to put a face on poverty in America. He later claimed that Lange exhibited an amazing sensitivity and rapport with people. She speculated that a pronounced limp from childhood polio often worked to her advantage, engendering sympathy and a bond with her subjects. At the end of her life, she included this piece in her final project, *Dorothea Lange Looks at the American Country Woman* (1967), wherein she linked the women's strength to their connection to the land: "These are women of the American soil. . . . They are of the roots of our country."

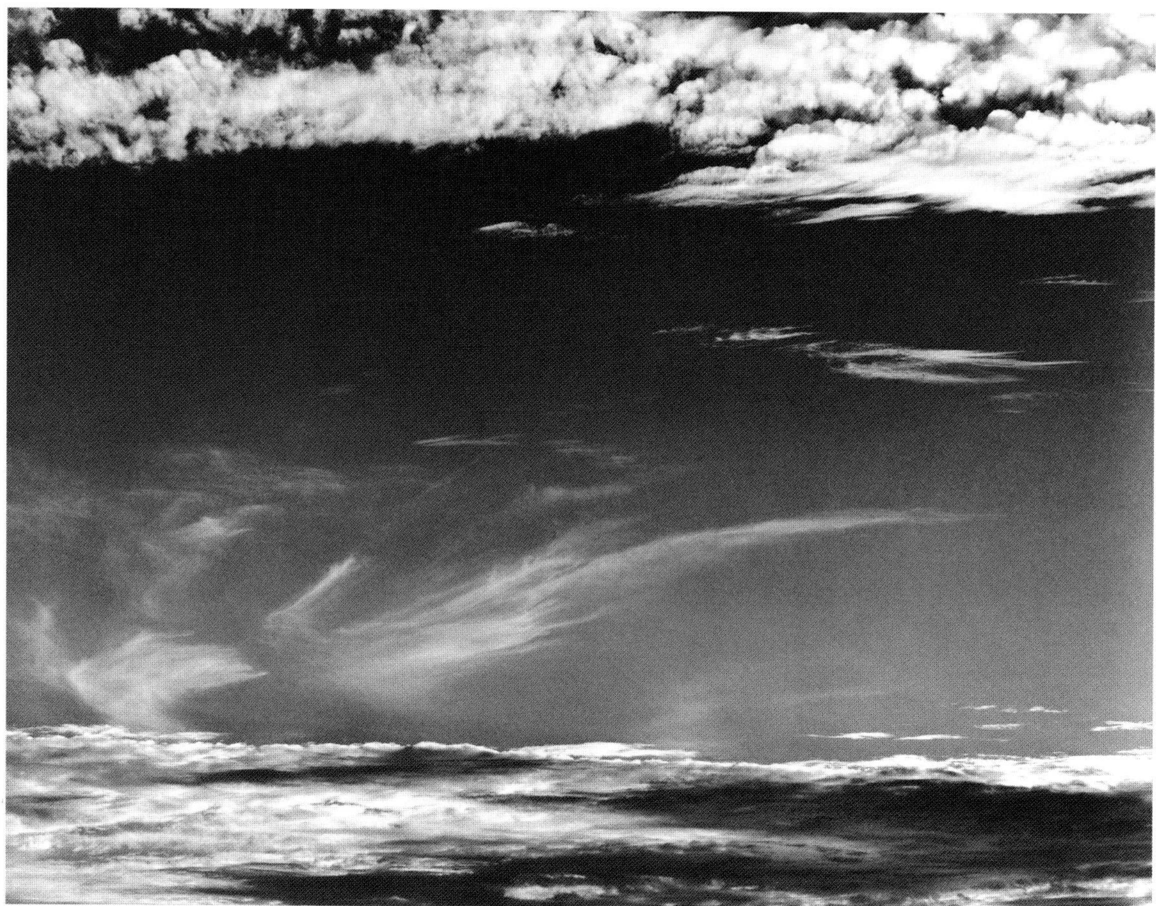

Edward Weston (1886–1958)

Clouds at Oceano, 1936
Gelatin silver print
7⅝ x 9⅝ in. (19.4 x 24.4 cm)

P1964.185

Between 1922 and 1931, influential American photographer and gallery director Alfred Stieglitz took hundreds of photographs of the sky. Rather than describe the sky, his goal was to create metaphors for his emotions. He called the works "equivalents." Edward Weston was strongly influenced by Stieglitz's approach to photography. When he met the master artist in 1922, Weston was on the cusp of shifting his allegiance from softly focused plays of painterly atmosphere to sharp-focus studies of the world's details. Stieglitz provided the final push.

When Weston took up the subject of sky and clouds in 1936, he was an established and influential artist respected for his spontaneous portraits; his evocative, even erotic, pictures of shells and vegetables; and his compositionally distilled nature studies and nudes. His hallmarks were crystalline printing and a focus on the beauty of object forms rendered in meticulous detail. Four years earlier, he had joined with his close friend Ansel Adams and a small number of respected California photographers to create an informal group called f-64, in celebration of the clarity and precision of the sharp, deep focus provided by that small aperture used on large view cameras. Now, besides turning his camera to the California sky, he captured sculpturally expressive studies of shifting sand dunes and full-body portraits of his lover, Charis Wilson, splayed nude across the sand. These subjects mark a broadening of his vision and a new commitment to subject over form.

Weston knew of Stieglitz's "equivalents" when he took his own sky photographs. But where Stieglitz had created brooding visions of the sun concealed behind banks of dense vapor, Weston delivered airy views of wispy light dancing across brilliantly clear space. Where Stieglitz reveled in dark phrases of abstract melody, Weston transformed the sky into spacious, effervescent landscapes.

Weston submitted this image to the John Simon Guggenheim Memorial Foundation in 1936 to accompany his fellowship application and became the first photographer to win that prestigious award. The award and a renewal in 1938 became the basis for Weston and Wilson's important collaborative book, *California and the West* (1940).

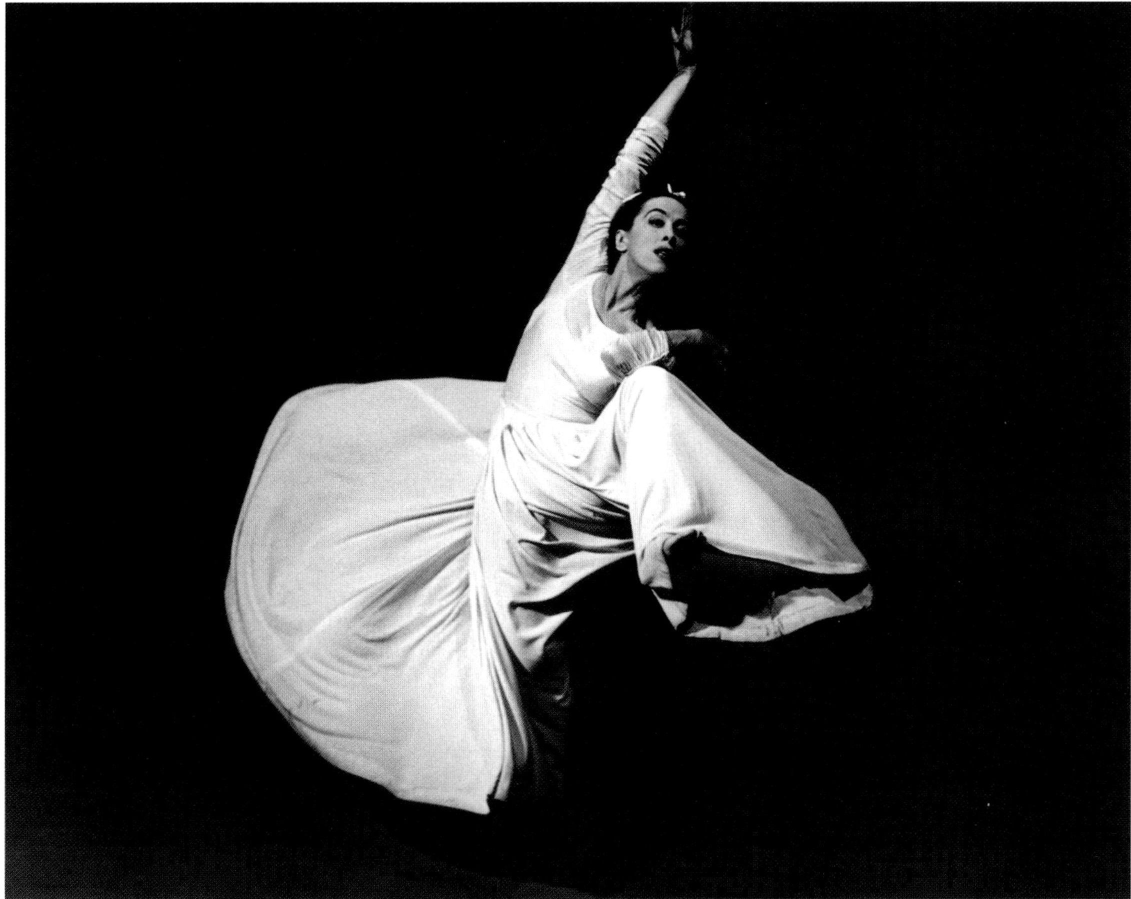

Barbara Morgan (1900–1992)

Martha Graham—Letter to the World (Swirl), 1940, print 1972
Gelatin silver print
13 9/16 x 10 5/16 in. (34.4 x 26.2 cm)

P1974.21.17

"Movement in the modern dance is the product not of invention but of discovery—discovery of what the body will do, and what it can do in the expression of emotions." So explained Martha Graham, one of the most influential dancers, teachers, and choreographers of the twentieth century, in Barbara Morgan's book *Martha Graham: Sixteen Dances in Photographs* (1941).

Trained as a painter, Morgan took up photography after the birth of her second child in 1935 because it offered a more flexible work schedule. But over the rest of her life, she applied the medium to create a challenging array of vibrant work that ranged from photomontage and light drawings to studies of nature. Her consistent goal was to use metaphor and rhythm to externalize and express "the invisible energies of life."

Morgan saw Graham dance for the first time the year that she committed herself to photography. Graham used dance in the same way that Southwest Indians did: to connect to earth's elemental forces and reflect humanity's inner character. This approach articulated Morgan's concept of meaningful art—that it be connected integrally to life. Graham soon found in Morgan an artist who had, as she later explained, the uncanny ability to "capture the instant of a dance and transform it into a timeless gesture." The two artists soon agreed to collaborate on a photographic project featuring the dancer in performance.

This photograph captures Graham late in the performance of *Letter to the World*, her tribute to the poet Emily Dickinson, after Dickinson has lost her lover and is in the midst of realizing that her happiness must be found in the intensity of her work. The performance's title and spoken words were from Dickinson's poems, and the dance sequence itself reflected the poet's maturation. But rather than present a strict biography, the dance reflects Dickinson's imagination, which Graham portrayed as tempestuous, in direct contrast to the poet's restrained exterior.

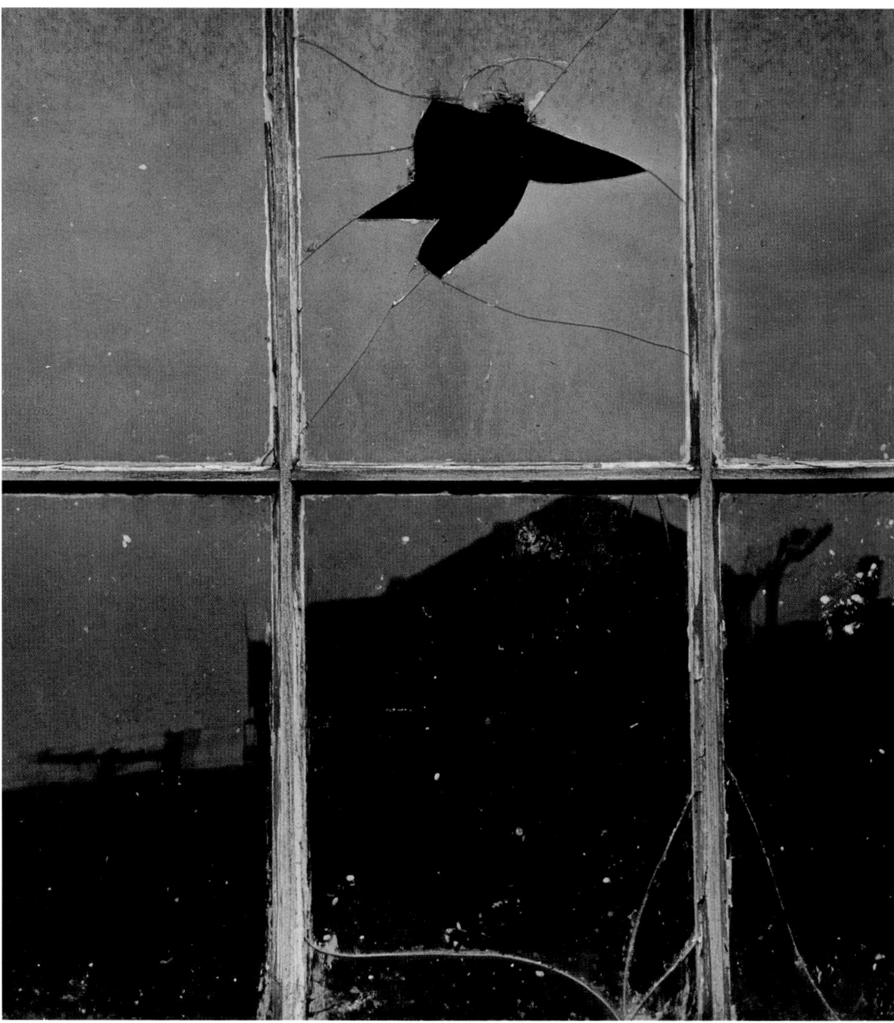

Aaron Siskind (1903–1991)

Gloucester, ca. 1944
Gelatin silver print
$8\frac{11}{16}$ x $7\frac{5}{8}$ in. (22 x 19.4 cm)

Courtesy Robert Mann Gallery, New York
P1997.40

Although Aaron Siskind's experience as a member of the New York-based Photo League was in the social documentary tradition, in the early 1940s he made an abrupt change and turned toward a more personal expressionistic style. As a high school English teacher, Siskind was inspired by literature and poetry to become more abstract and metaphorical with his photography. Additionally, while living in Greenwich Village—the hotbed of New York's art activity in the 1940s—Siskind spent his evenings with artists discussing their desire to find a new form of expression. He discovered that he felt more of an affinity with abstract-expressionist painters than he did with photographers. Becoming friends with artists like Barnett Newman, Adolph Gottlieb, and Mark Rothko, Siskind was soon experimenting with transforming the substance of the world into poetic imagery.

In 1943 Siskind went to Gloucester, Massachusetts, for part of the summer, where he had what he later described as a photographic epiphany. He began to experiment with ways to let the subject matter become less important and instead strove for a visceral feeling brought on by viewing the image. He returned in the summer of 1944 and continued to develop the ideas begun the previous year. Although he still used a view camera to render objects with sharp detail and crisp texture, Siskind concentrated more on shapes in isolation and the relationships between them to create the meaning of the image. Successfully blending aesthetic form and content, he created a new pictorial iconography.

In this image, one of his earliest created during this period of experimentation, Siskind used the cross shapes of the window frame, the dark reflections on the lower panels, and the ghostly form created by the negative space of the broken glass to conjure up a dark dreamscape.

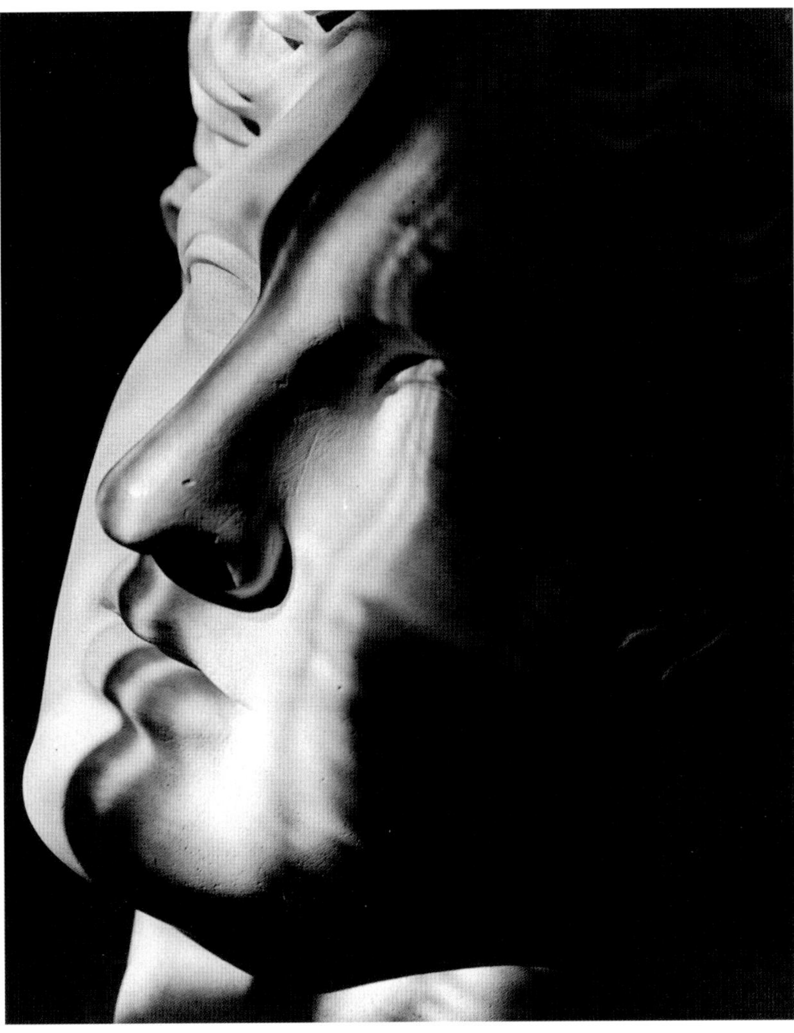

Carlotta Corpron (1901–1988)

Illusion of Male and Female, 1946, print 1976
Gelatin silver print
13 3/16 x 10 3/8 in. (33.5 x 26.4 cm)
Copyright 1988, Amon Carter Museum, Fort Worth, Texas,
Gift of the Dorothea Leonhardt Fund of the Communities Foundation of Texas, Inc., Dallas, Texas
P1985.2.30

When Carlotta Corpron made this study of shadows on a plaster cast, her primary intent was to demonstrate to her students creative ways to illustrate the effects of light. She had been teaching design and art for twenty years, the last ten of them at Texas Women's College in Denton, where she stayed until 1968. She only learned photography in 1936, when college officials asked her to teach a course in it, but she immediately became obsessed with the medium and experimented with it for about a decade.

Most of her work explored principles of design and grew out of her classes, since she taught by her own example. In trying to illustrate how light gives shape to form, she assigned her students an exercise to use a plaster cast as a subject. For her own contribution, she made three exposures, demonstrating the entirely different effects made by variations in lighting. In this image, the shadow creates a second profile, revealing the illusion of two figures superimposed, one with more sensuous rounded curves and one with severe lines producing a more angular profile.

Although Corpron photographed intensively for only a brief period, she was one of the few photographers in the country to focus on abstraction. She quickly gained a reputation for her innovative approach and concentration on light as subject matter. Both Lázsló Moholy-Nagy and Gyorgy Kepes, who taught at Chicago's School of Design, visited Denton in the early 1940s to teach workshops and were impressed with her work. In a letter to Corpron, Kepes praised her for "hand[ling] light with freedom and understanding as a good sculptor handles clay. You really mold your photographs from light."

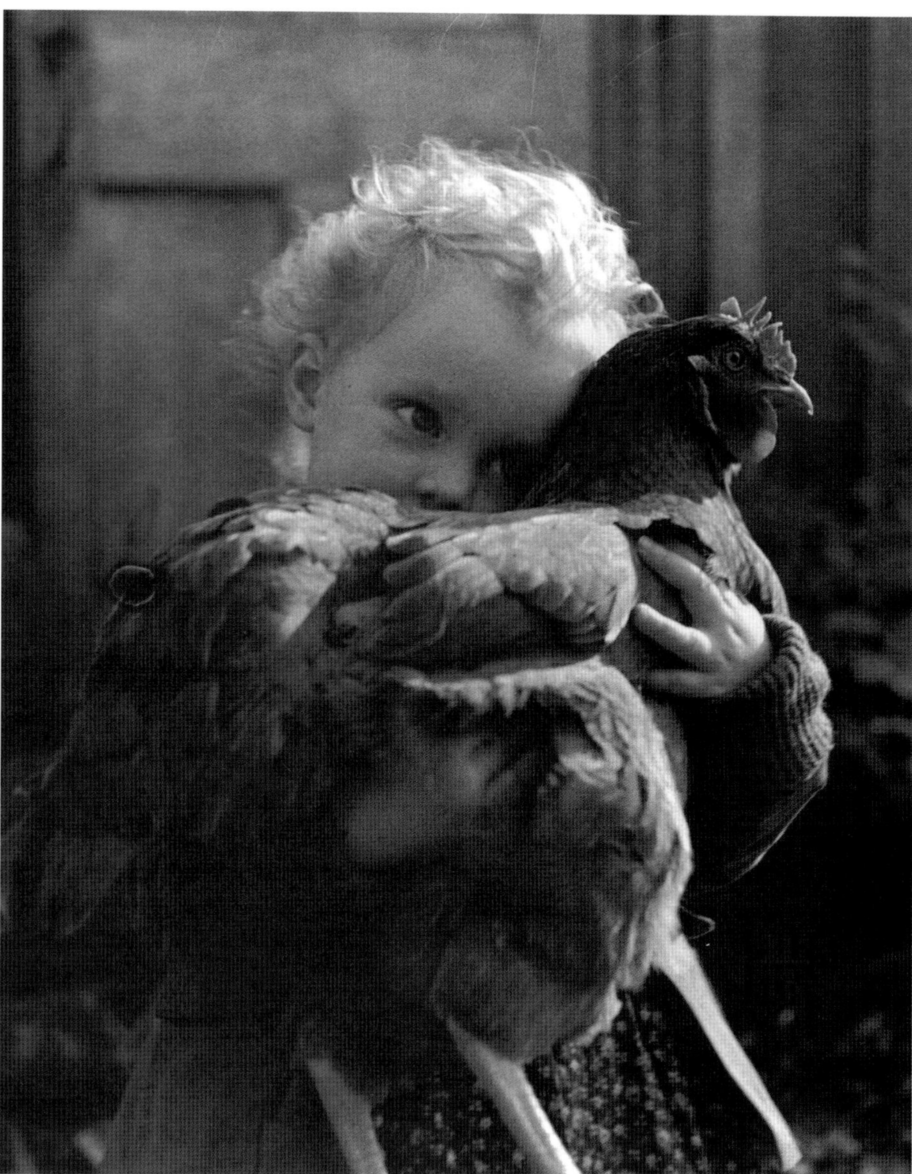

Nell Dorr
(1893–1989)
Bethany Holding Chicken, 1942–43,
print ca. 1964
Gelatin silver print
19¾ x 15⅞ in. (50.2 x 40.3 cm)

Gift of the Estate of Nell Dorr
P1990.45.72

While their husbands were all serving in the military during World War II, photographer Nell Dorr, along with her daughters and their children, moved into a country home in New England. With no thought of ever publishing the photographs, Dorr made pictures of their experiences there in an attempt to capture the sweet moments of mothers watching their children grow. Only after one of her daughters died did she go back and look through the images and select those with universal meaning, sequencing them to celebrate the bond between mother and child. When she published her pictorialist masterpiece, *Mother and Child* (1954), Dorr believed that the traditional image of motherhood was losing status in America, as many women apologized for being "just a mother," and she wanted her soft-focus images to communicate the spiritual essence of the mother-child relationship. The United States Information Agency distributed 1,000 copies of the book to libraries around the world to counteract Cold War depictions of American women as lazy and dependent on modern conveniences.

Dorr's good friend, children's book illustrator Tasha Tudor, frequently visited with her young children as she looked for a country home in the same area, so her family appears in many of the photographs. Tudor ironically remembered that she first fell in love with farm life when she was living in New York City and had adopted a rescued chicken. Her daughter Bethany remembered loving the chickens in the yard at Dorr's home and enjoyed having them sit on her shoulder or cuddle in her lap. Dorr captured a moment when the young child held one of the chickens in a loving embrace, much as she would a stuffed animal. In her book, Dorr placed a poem before this section in which she spoke of the joys of raising children and of seeing the promise in their eyes.

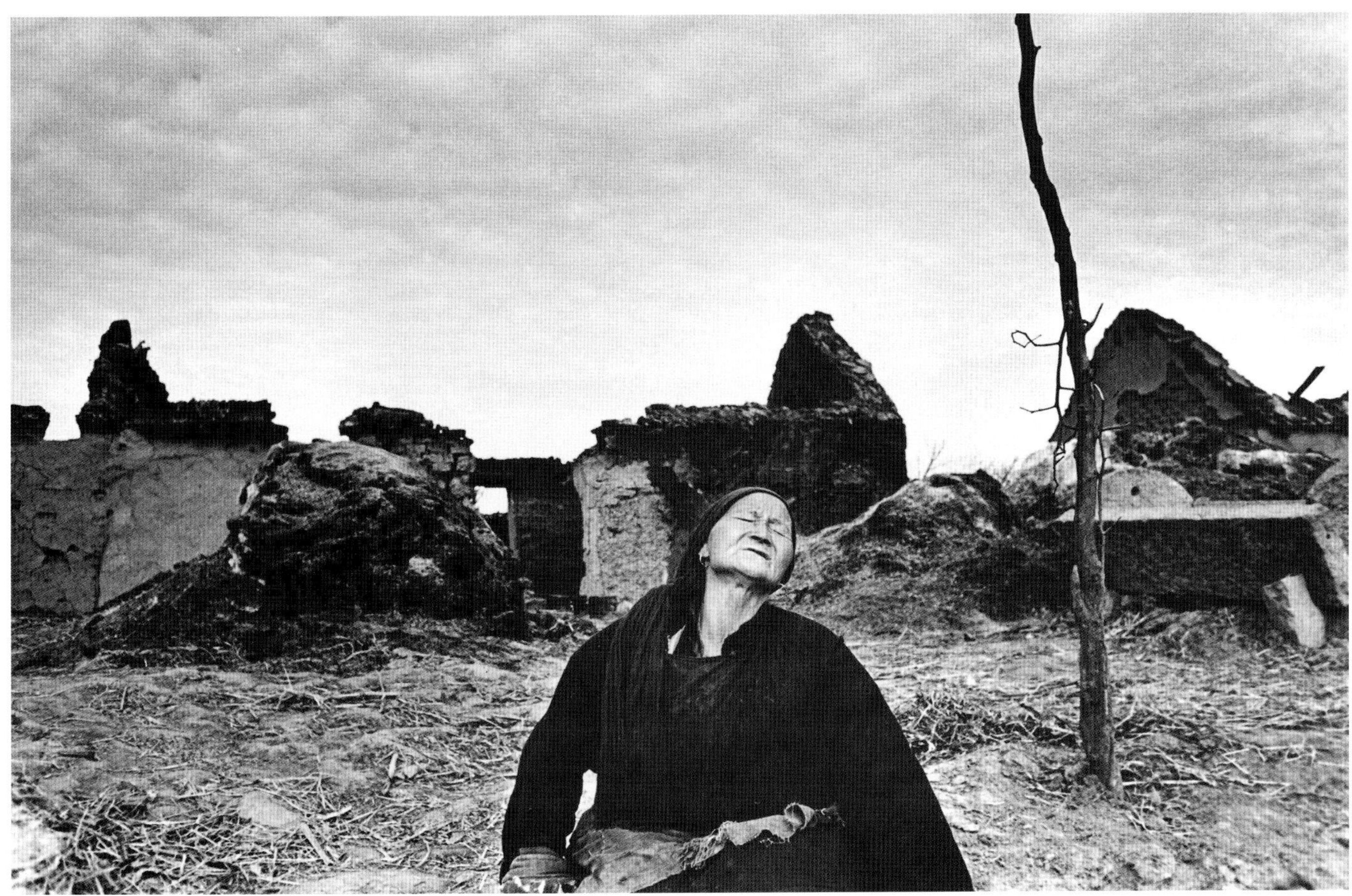

Carl Mydans (b. 1907)

Sole Survivor of a Village near Pengpu, China, Mourns in the Ruins after the Civil War Passed Through in December, 1948, print 1985
Gelatin silver print
20 x 29 13/16 in. (50.8 x 75.7 cm)
 Gift of Time Inc., New York, New York
P1985.27.49

Carl Mydans photographed this grieving woman while documenting the aftermath of the Communists' advance from their control points in northern China through the southern areas held by the Nationalists. A photojournalist for over fifty years, Mydans is best known for his documentation of the Pacific theatre in World War II and the Korean War. He photographed combat throughout three decades. He began his career, however, as a peacetime documentary photographer, working for the Farm Security Administration before leaving to work for the new magazine called *Life* in 1936. This period greatly influenced his photojournalistic style, and, although he would record important historical moments, he approached the task as a humanist narrating a personal story. Describing himself as an obsessive people watcher, he focused on expressive faces in order to relate the story of an individual trapped by the circumstances of war.

Mydans became Time-Life bureau chief in Tokyo in 1947. The following year, he went to China to cover the conclusion of the civil war. Wanting to find an area of combat on the frontlines, he traveled to the area of Xuzhou, where the decisive campaign of the war had left over half a million casualties on each side in late 1948. There, he found no formal frontline, only pockets of independent forces dug in or moving on. The rural villages in the Anhwei region had changed hands many times during the fighting, leaving the villagers devastated and feeling betrayed by both sides. Most villages were completely shelled. What structures remained had been commandeered, and all the livestock and food had been eaten by the soldiers. In this remarkable image of a village's lone survivor, Mydans included enough of the background rubble to convey the village's destruction—a fitting backdrop to the devastation and anguish in the woman's face.

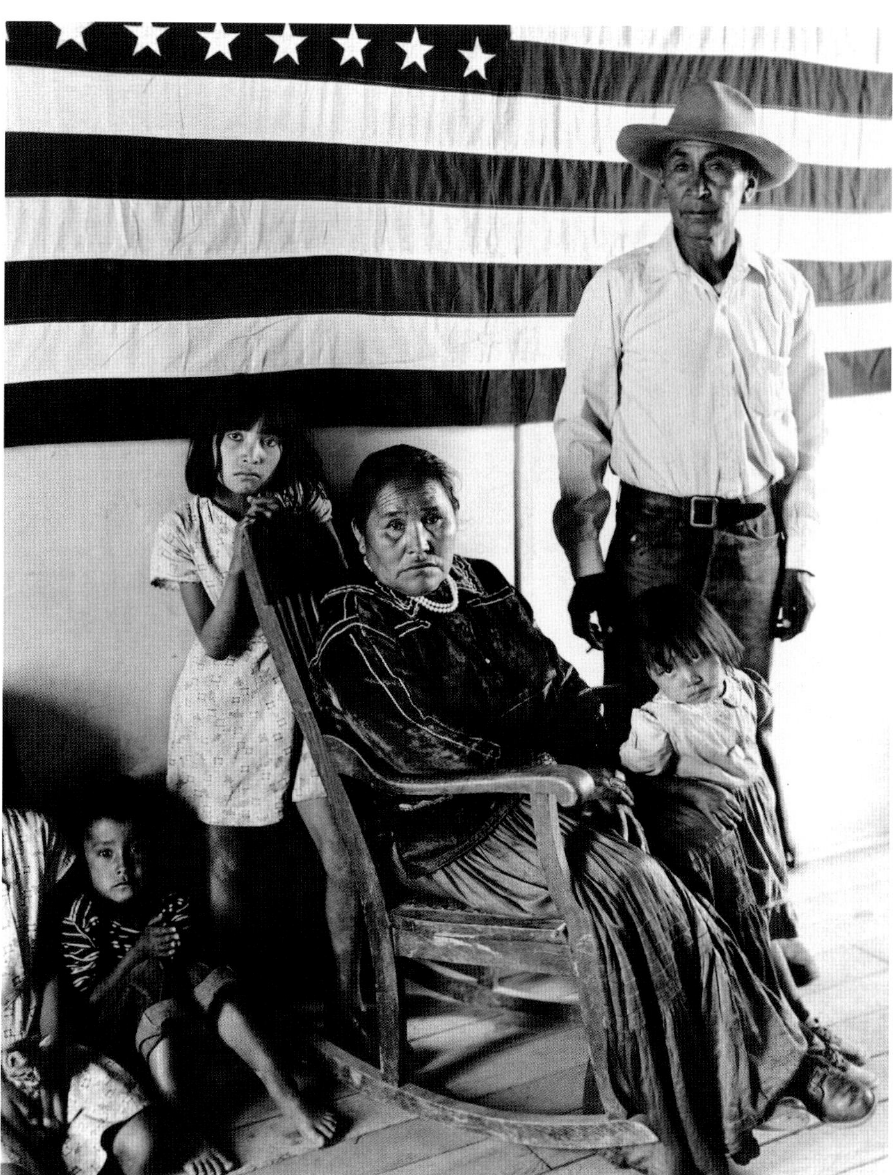

Laura Gilpin (1891–1979)

Navaho Family [Francis Nakai and family, Red Rock], 1950
Gelatin silver print
13¼ x 10¾ in. (34.9 x 27.3 cm)
Copyright 1979, Amon Carter Museum, Fort Worth, Texas, Gift of the artist
P1979.95.15

Although this photograph dates from 1950, Gilpin first photographed the Nakai family in 1932, the year she began her lifelong project to document the Navajo people and lands. She visited the area over the next year and a half, while her friend Betsy Forster worked for the New Mexico Association on Indian Affairs as a field nurse in the small Navajo community of Red Rock. The Nakais were Forster's neighbors and since Francis Nakai was one of the few Navajo who spoke English at that time, he frequently acted as the photographer's guide. Gilpin returned to the reservation in the 1950s and documented the Navajo society, illustrating both the traditional ways and the changes that modern society had brought.

The Nakai family figures prominently in the book Gilpin published on the Navajo, and she discussed the occasion of this portrait in the epilogue to *The Enduring Navaho* (1968). Gilpin explained that the flag behind the group had draped the coffin of the oldest Nakai boy, who was killed in Europe while serving in World War II.

The war was a major turning point for the Navajo, who rallied in huge numbers to defend their country, their land, and their people. The war effort provided unprecedented opportunities for employment, both in military service and war-related jobs, and it also introduced many Navajo to the outside world for the first time. By photographing the Nakai family against the American flag, Gilpin resurrected the nineteenth-century style of positioning Native Americans against a background of Navajo rugs and symbolized their integration into American society.

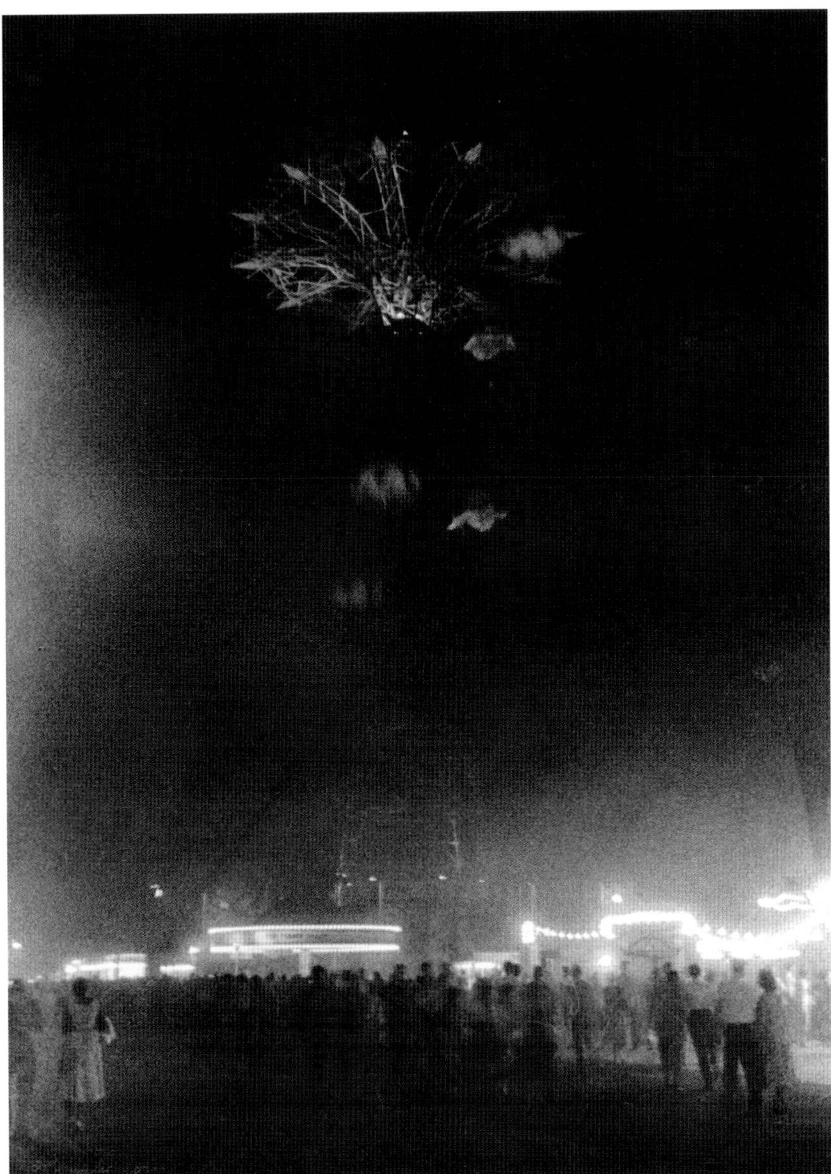

Robert Frank
(b. 1924)

Fourth of July, 1958, Coney Island, 1958
Gelatin silver print
16⅞ x 14 in. (42.9 x 35.6 cm)
Copyright Robert Frank, Courtesy Pace/MacGill Gallery, New York
P1997.22

When Swiss-born Robert Frank photographed Coney Island on the southwest tip of Brooklyn in 1958, the Steeplechase amusement park with its iconic Parachute Jump was definitely past its prime and represented the seedy side of American popular culture. Built in 1897, Steeplechase Park was the first of three amusement parks to provide cheap entertainment for New York City's middle and lower classes. The 262-foot-tall Parachute Jump tower was added in 1941. Throughout the 1940s and 1950s, the park deteriorated steadily and increasingly attracted crime and violence. Six years after Frank made this image, the park was closed and all rides were destroyed except for the Parachute Jump, which proved too expensive to demolish. Photographing the park at night, with only the lights of the rides and gaming booths for illumination, Frank evoked a feeling of surreal danger in the ghostly scene.

Coney Island was one of two projects Frank completed that year as he awaited publication of the work he had concluded during a year's travel throughout America on a 1955 and 1956 Guggenheim Fellowship. His provocative French publication *Les Americains* (1958, followed in 1959 by the American version, *The Americans*) created an uproar among critics and was radically influential on later generations of photographers. Frank's visual style—which emphasized the qualities of the hand-held camera through the use of natural light, exaggerated grain, and blurred detail—revolutionized photographic aesthetics with its expressive, improvisational look. Additionally, the photographer moved away from a supposedly objective documentary style and photographed in a self-consciously subjective manner. He highlighted what he saw as the worst aspects of American popular culture and materialism and depicted an anonymous mass society overpowering the individual. Although the 1950s were typically thought of as a happy decade, Frank brought an outsider's perspective and predicted the issues that would explode in the 1960s: alienation, racism, disillusionment with politics, and the growing restlessness among the nation's youth.

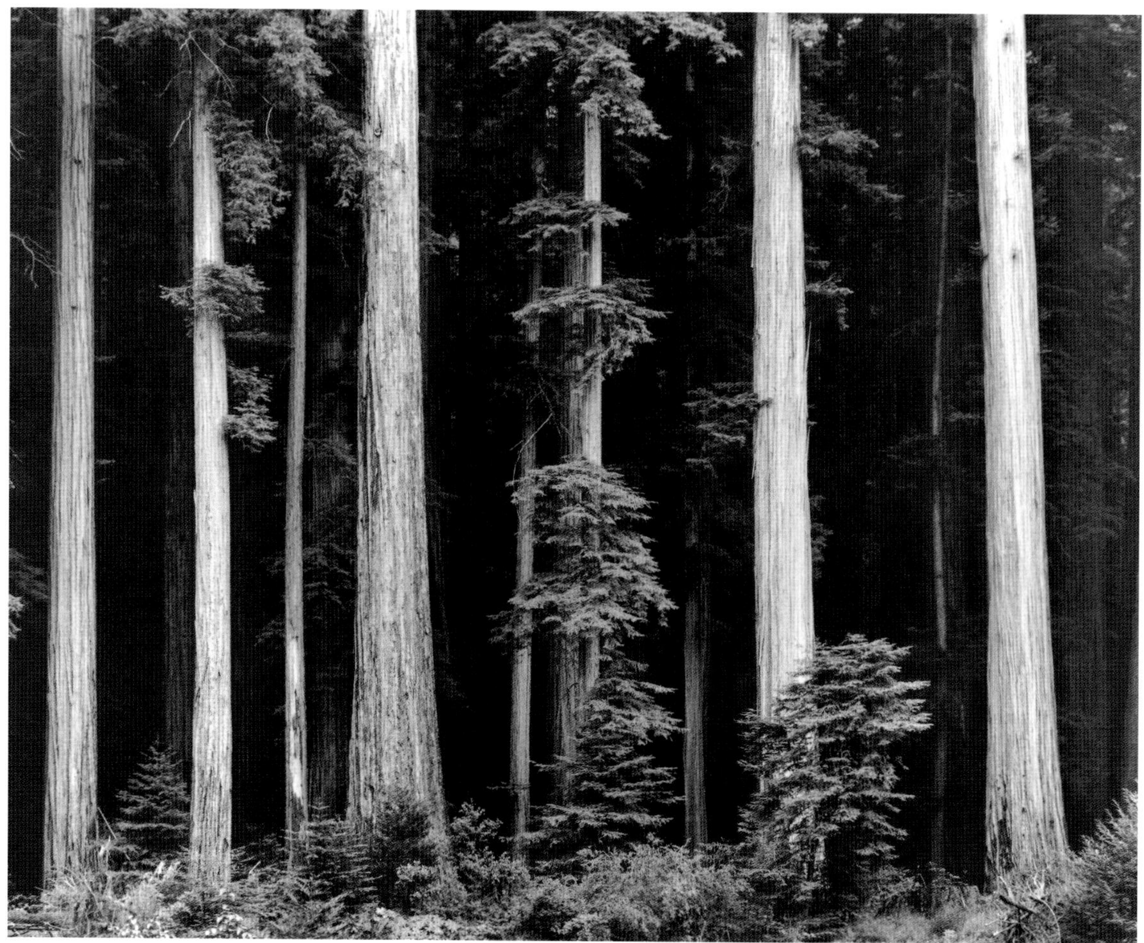

Ansel Adams (1902–1984)

Northern California Coast Redwoods [Bull Creek Flat, California], ca. 1960, print 1963
Gelatin silver print
9 7/16 x 11 1/2 in. (23.9 x 29.1 cm)

P1966.11.10

When Ansel Adams photographed this grove, both he and the redwoods were clearly associated with the environmental movement in America. Occasionally growing to more than 360 feet, northern California coast redwoods are the tallest living things on earth and can survive for thousands of years. With massive trunks and shallow root systems, the trees only grow naturally in the moist, mild climate of that coastal region, so when conservationists witnessed logging operations moving towards this great forest in 1917, they established the Save-the-Redwoods League. In 1921, with the addition of state funds, the league purchased its first grove, now part of the Humboldt Redwoods State Park, where these trees stand. Shortly thereafter, John D. Rockefeller Jr. brought his family to Bull Creek Flat and subsequently made a $2 million donation to the league to help purchase 9,000 acres. However, clear-cut logging in the headwaters of Bull Creek in the 1940s and 1950s triggered disastrous erosion along the waterway. During the major floods of 1955 and 1964, hundreds of "saved" redwoods fell. Conservation of the nation's natural resources was clearly more complex than just saving trees from being cut.

To Adams, wilderness was a source of divine inspiration and should be experienced by everyone, emotionally and intellectually. He saw his photographs as an equivalent of what he saw and felt, and through publishing them, he could share his appreciation of the natural world and promote a message of preservation. Adams included a print of this image in the 1963 portfolio, *What Majestic Word*, published by the Sierra Club in commemoration of Russell Varian, a longtime supporter who gave much of his earnings to the protection of the coast redwoods.

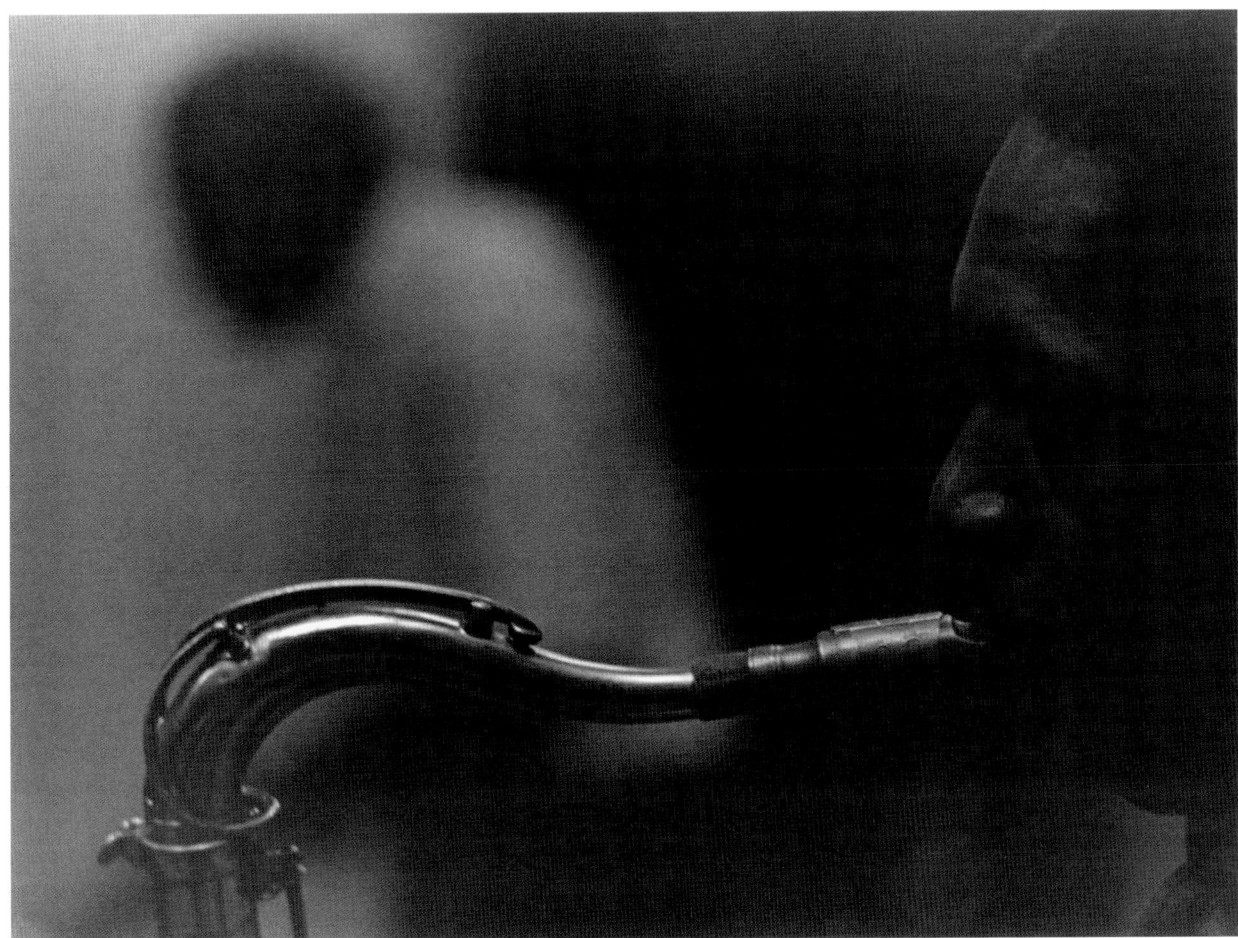

Roy DeCarava (b. 1919)

Coltrane and Elvin, New York, 1960, print 1982
Gelatin silver print
10 1/16 x 13 in. (25.5 x 33 cm)

P1991.13.2

Raised in Harlem, Roy DeCarava interpreted that neighborhood with an insider's perspective. The first black photographer to receive a Guggenheim Fellowship, he combined his expressive images with text by the poet Langston Hughes in the critically acclaimed book *The Sweet Flypaper of Life* (1955).

As an outgrowth of that project, the photographer set out to turn his camera on the world of jazz. DeCarava found inspiration in the musicians' total commitment to their art and believed that for them, the object was not so much the performance as it was the experience of plumbing the self. His photographs depict musicians in isolated concentration, self-absorbed in the act of creation. Regretting that he never photographed the saxophonist Charlie Parker, DeCarava committed himself to photographing John Coltrane and attended his performances throughout the Northeast whenever he could. Coltrane formed his own quartet in April 1960, and drummer Elvin Jones joined the band just prior to the October Atlantic recording session that resulted in Coltrane's now landmark album *My Favorite Things.*

DeCarava drew parallels between jazz and photography, seeing both as expressive art forms rich in metaphor. He favored the hand-held camera for its ability to respond immediately to everyday experience and believed that form, rather than subject matter, imparts emotional and psychological meaning. Just as jazz improvisation is a moment-to-moment, expressive interplay between musical voices, he too could intuitively choose a particular interplay between the different visual voices of light, shape, shadow, and plane. Preferring emotional atmosphere to detail, DeCarava is known for his luxurious shadows and interplay between tones at the lower end of the photographic scale. This photograph of Coltrane and Jones is constructed like a musical duet with Coltrane and his horn upfront and Jones in the background providing rhythm. The highlights of the horn define the melody, which courses through the composition in fluid harmony.

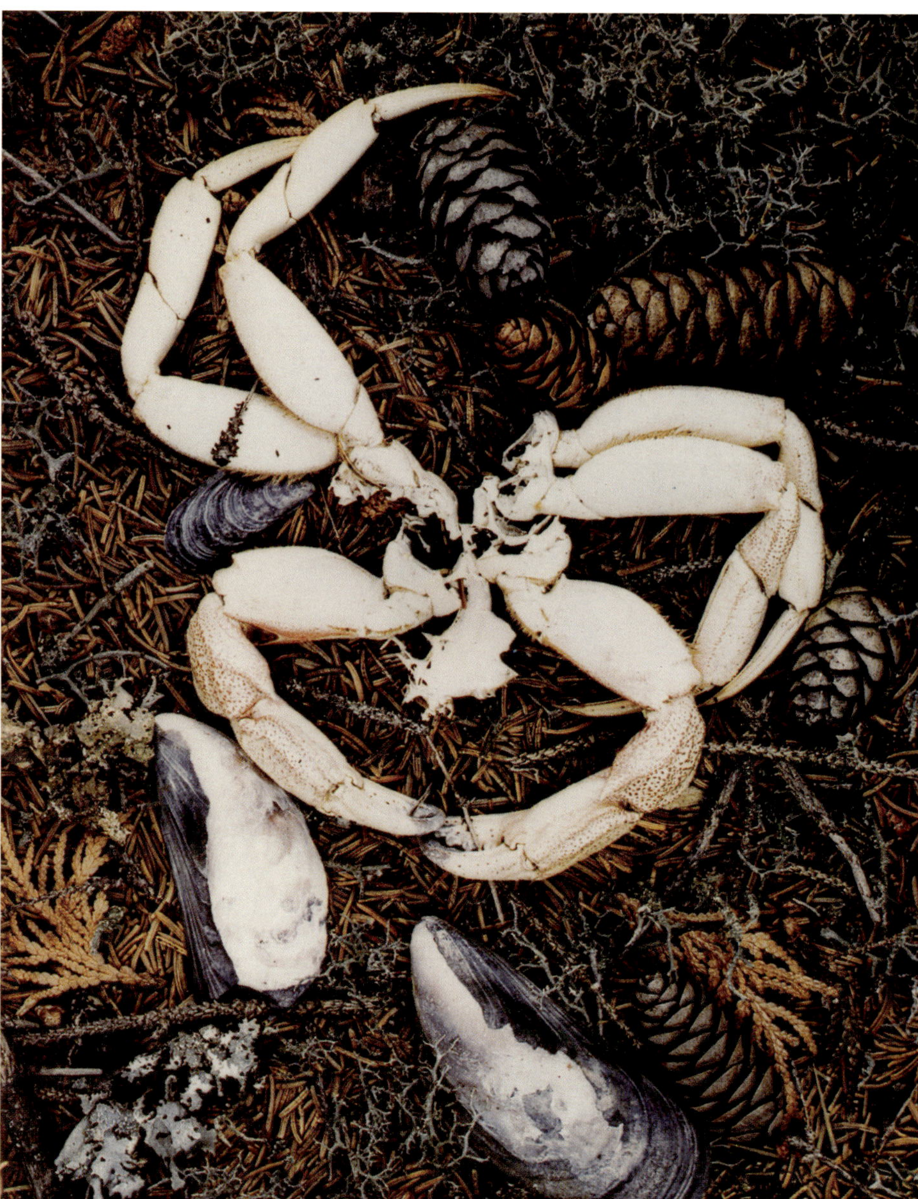

Eliot Porter
(1901–1990)

Crab Legs Left by Crows, Great Spruce Head Island, Maine, July 17, 1949, 1949
10⅝ x 8⅛ in. (27 x 20.6 cm)
Copyright 1990, Amon Carter Museum, Fort Worth, Texas, Bequest of Eliot Porter
P1990.51.2996.2

Eliot Porter played a pioneering role in cultivating public appreciation for the expressive capabilities of color photography. Committing himself to the medium in 1940, long before it was widely accepted, he established a vibrant model for nature photography. He used that model to help establish a broad-based environmental movement and draw attention to the astonishing variety of nature's forms and colors.

Porter trained to be a medical doctor and took up a career as a researcher in biochemistry. But he found the lure of making photographs, a childhood hobby, more appealing than the laboratory. When, in late 1938, the important photographer and dealer Alfred Stieglitz exhibited Porter's black-and-white photographic close-ups of birds and nature landscapes at his New York City gallery, 291, Porter quit his medical work to take up photography full time.

Stieglitz's acclaim catapulted Porter into the ranks of the finest artists, on a par with Paul Strand and Ansel Adams. Yet rather than build directly on that foundation, Porter immediately took up the new, unexplored field of color. This early picture of a crabshell lying on the forest floor strikingly illustrates Porter's remarkable penchant for creating unexpectedly evocative visions of overlooked objects in nature. Captured at his family's summer retreat on the Maine coast, this image illuminates the beauty found in weathered decay, drawing implicit references to nature's fundamental cycling of life and death. The subtle browns, greens, blues, and oranges of the print add to the image's realism while heightening awareness of nature's varied hues. Indeed, Porter was a master at teasing out color to enhance the emotional effect of his compositions. Delicate photographs like this drew the attention and respect of Porter's colleagues and, by the early 1960s, the acclaim of a broad public. Such images serve as persuasive reminders to slow down and study the unexpected beauty of nature's ever-changing array.

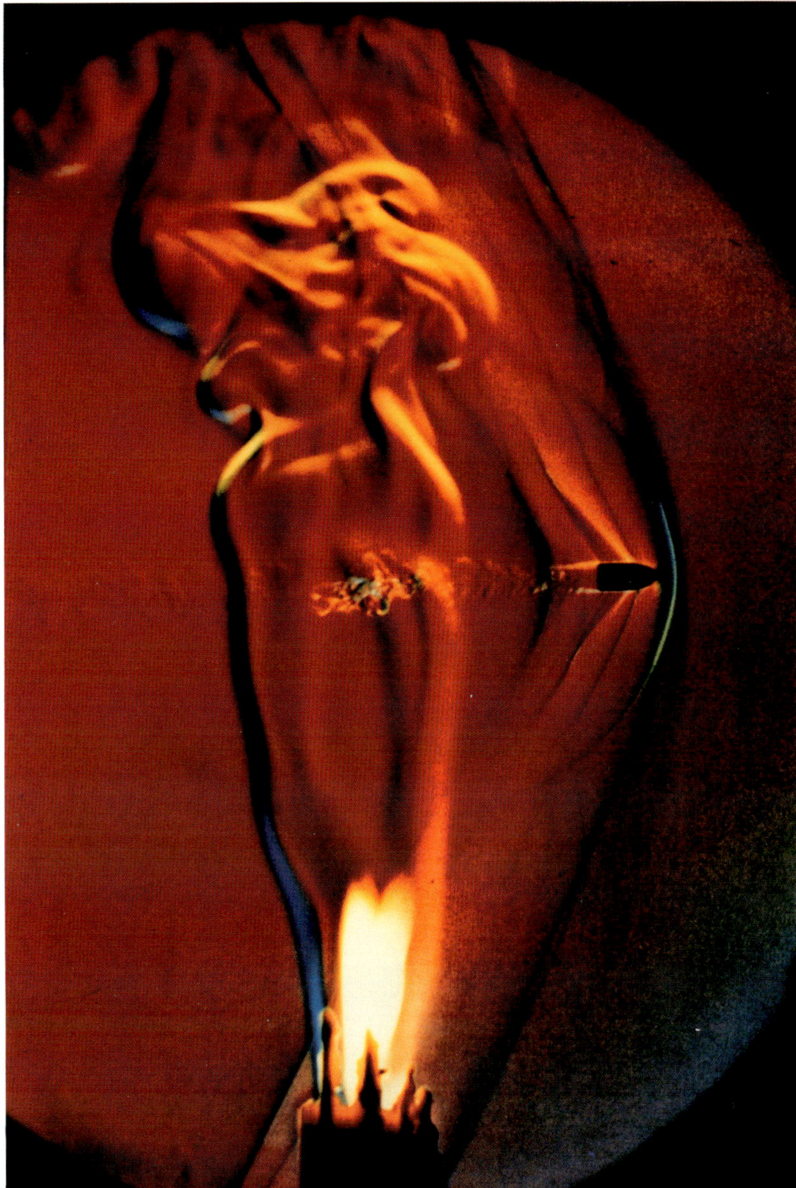

Harold E. Edgerton (1903–1990) and J. Kim Vandiver (b. 1945)

Bullet thru Flame, 1973
Dye coupler print
18¼ x 12$^{3}/_{16}$ in. (46.4 x 31 cm)

Gift of James P. Harrington, West Chester, Pennsylvania
P1985.46

Harold Edgerton had been making photographs of moving objects for more than forty years when he and his Massachusetts Institute of Technology research assistant, Kim Vandiver, created this image. Perfecting the modern stroboscope in 1931 to assess the vibration of high-speed machinery, Edgerton found a career in blending the worlds of art and industry by applying his invention to creating ultrahigh-speed photographs of objects in motion. In so doing, he took the motion studies of Eadweard Muybridge and Etienne-Jules Marey to their logical next step by extending human vision to the microsecond.

Edgerton photographed a wide array of subjects, from a coronet made by a drop of milk to the impact of a kicker's boot on a football. But one of his favorite subjects was a bullet passing through or striking different materials. He photographed bullets bisecting playing cards, rupturing balloons, and decimating apples with one-millionth-of-a-second flash exposures. He revealed that a bullet entering a lightbulb causes the bulb's far side to crack before the bullet arrives there. Under Edgerton's direction, Vandiver created this photograph to record the shock waves of a bullet as it travels through space. Using a special technique called Schlieren photography, which records the deflected patterns of disturbed gases, the spectacular speed of a bullet is arrested the instant it passes above a candle's flame.

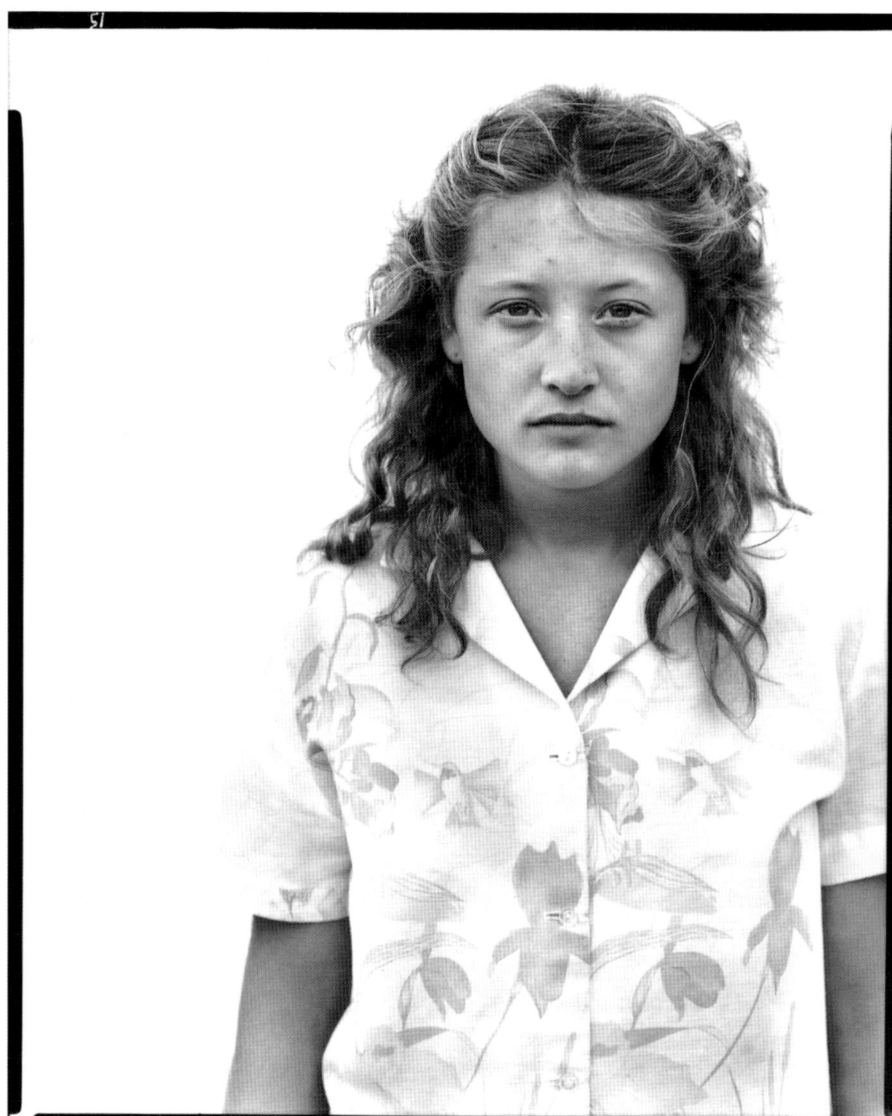

Richard Avedon (b. 1923)

Shawna Callahan, Thirteen Year Old, Cheyenne, Wyoming, 7/30/82, 1985
Gelatin silver print mounted to aluminum panel
$56\frac{1}{4}$ x $45\frac{1}{4}$ in. (142.8 x 114.3 cm)

P1985.28.8

Renowned portrait, reportage, and fashion photographer Richard Avedon photographed this young girl during a six-year project photographing working-class people of the American West, whom he described as the hidden strength of the country. Although originally concerned that his New York City background might prohibit his success at portraying people outside his frame of reference, after photographing a rancher in Montana, Avedon realized that it is the shared elements in life that foster understanding. Former Amon Carter Museum Director Mitchell Wilder was impressed by the fresh perspective that Avedon brought to his portrait of the rancher. In an unprecedented move for an art museum, in 1979 the Carter underwrote the photographer's task of interpreting the unsung people of the American West.

Working primarily in daylight during the spring and fall months, Avedon visited locations where he would find appropriate subjects for his portraits, including both worksites, such as mines and factories, and recreational sites, like regional festivals and fairs. The photographer isolated his subjects against a sheet of white, seamless paper to concentrate on the people that inspired him, rather than on the western locale. His large view camera produced eight-by-ten-inch negatives that hold their sharp details in larger-than-life prints, inviting close study of the wonders of human diversity. Throughout the project, the photographer exposed 17,000 sheets of film during 752 individual sittings. Never intended to be objective documents of the West, the portraits are instead an evocative record of the photographer's responses to the people he photographed. Avedon found the windblown and sun-bleached Shawna Callahan at Cheyenne's Frontier Days, one of the country's oldest and largest rodeos. The thirteen-year-old confronts the viewer with an unflinching and disarming directness that belies her youth.

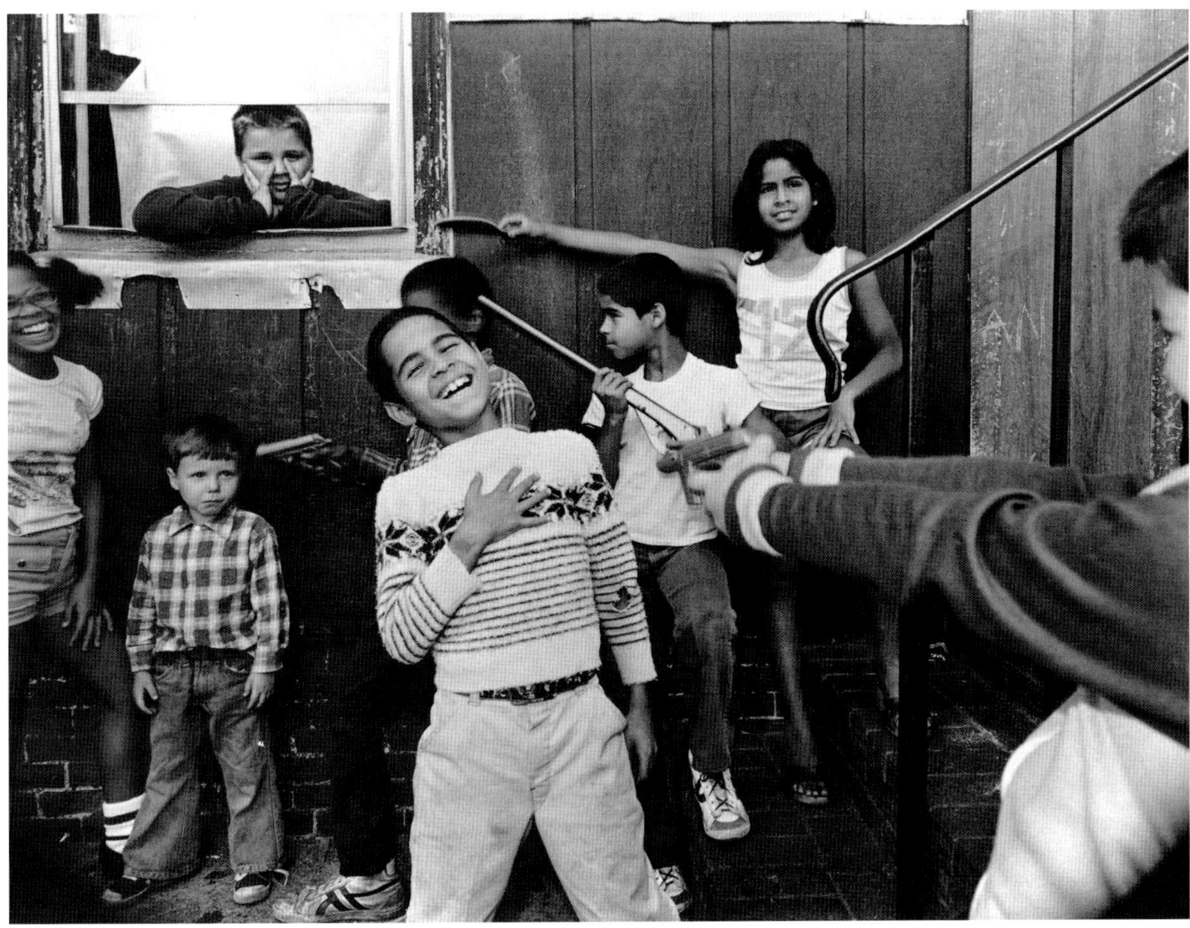

Nicholas Nixon (b. 1947)

Chelsea, Massachusetts, 1981
Gelatin silver print
7 11/16 x 9 11/16 in. (19.5 x 24.6 cm)

P1983.43.1

In the late 1970s and 1980s, Nicholas Nixon helped lead a revival of the use of the large-format view camera and meticulously crafted contact print. This came decades after the fine art photography field had been dominated by the aesthetic of the 35mm hand-held camera. In his "front porch" series, made between 1977 and 1982, the photographer employed the eight-by-ten-inch camera in an atypical manner by incorporating the spontaneity of the hand-held camera to capture intricately choreographed groups of people. Nixon further intensified the visual complexity by using a wide-angle lens that increased the depth of focus and allowed him to photograph large groups at close range, creating distortion at the image edges.

The front porch series mixes Nixon's formal concerns with an egalitarian social sensibility. He walked throughout Boston when he was most likely to find people outside, gathered on the porches and stoops. Because the cumbersome equipment made his photographic activity obvious, the images required his subjects' cooperation and active participation. Following an interest in narrative, Nixon allowed his unidentified subjects to act out stories or strike dramatic poses.

Chelsea, an industrial suburb just north of Boston with a diverse population, provided the photographer with the working-class neighborhood he favored. The laughter in this image implies that all is make believe, but the violence depicted is deeply unsettling. The path of pretend gunfire ends with the smallest child, whose serious gaze asks the viewer to consider the consequences of such gunplay.

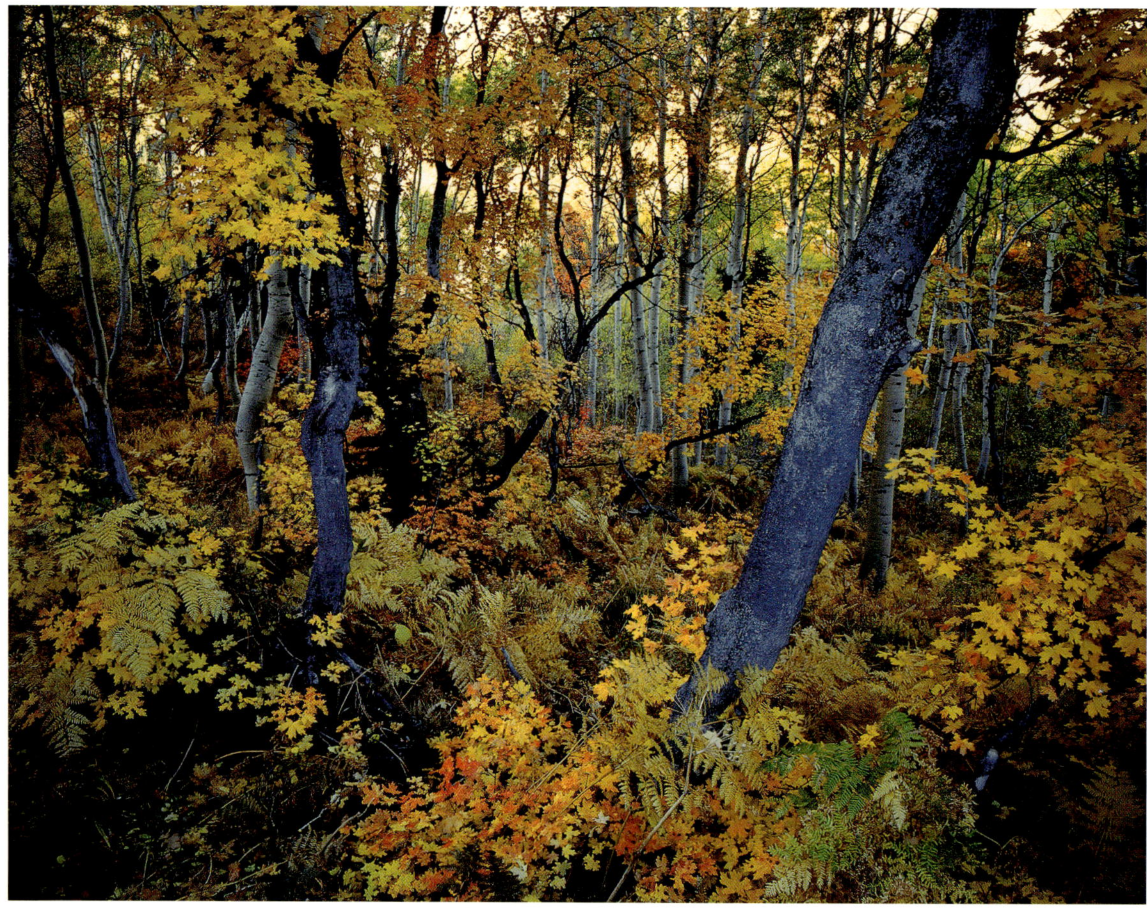

Robert Glenn Ketchum (b. 1947)

Cosmic Trees, 1988
Dye destruction print
29½ x 37⅛ in. (74.9 x 94.3 cm)
Copyright 1988, Robert Glenn Ketchum, Gift of Herb Belkin
P1997.54

Robert Glenn Ketchum was inspired by Eliot Porter's example to trade a career in graphic design for the less-certain world of color landscape photography. He is now one of America's premiere nature photographers. Like Porter, Ketchum brings a strong environmentalist stance to his work. Following his mentor's path, he compiles captivating visual portraits of specific places, assembling sets of stunningly colorful exhibition prints as the foundations for books. The resulting volumes, including *The Hudson River and the Highlands* (1982), *The Tongass: Alaska's Vanishing Rain Forest* (1987), and *Overlooked in America: The Success and Failure of Federal Land Management* (1991), draw explicit attention to lands challenged by human defilement, revealing both the beauty and the degradation inscribing these places.

While Ketchum's intellect draws attention to our effective divorce from the natural world, his eye and emotions are subsumed within a vision of transcendentalist beauty, where light, color, form, and texture are melded in meticulous balance. *Cosmic Trees* provides a resplendent example of his approach. Part of Ketchum's *Sundance Suite,* the image records a magical sight that exceeds believability, where the electric blue of the maple and aspen tree trunks seems to float to the surface in captivating complement to the intricate patternings of the surrounding leaves. The effect is surreal, built on dreamlike wonder and filled with implicit action, much like an abstract expressionist painting. Ketchum explains in his book *The Legacy of Wildness* (1993), "I am often asked whether I see myself as an artist or an environmental activist. In looking back over all of this work, I think that I am a colorist. Regardless of my concerns, formal or political, regardless of the context of the work and the words by which I define these individual ideas and projects, all of them are united by a single pervasive interest that overrides all others—my use of color."

Robert Adams (b. 1937)

Southwest from South Jetty, 1990, print 1995
Gelatin silver print
14 7/16 x 18 1/8 in. (36.7 x 46 cm)
Copyright Robert Adams
P1998.62

Robert Adams writes, "Of all the sacred places on the coast, none is more comforting than where rivers join the sea. By the rivers' disappearance we are reminded of life's passing, while by the ocean's beauty we accept it, in a hope we cannot explain." Like Robert Glenn Ketchum, Adams has long voiced concern over America's despoliation of its land. But where Ketchum visualizes his concern in oversized photographs of resplendent color, Adams remains firmly committed to the graphic beauty of black and white.

Southwest from South Jetty comes from Adams' extended photographic homage to the mouth of the Columbia River near his Oregon home. The westernmost reach of Lewis and Clark's frontier explorations, this site, the artist suggests, is a place where one can turn away from the deforestation and commercial development that are fast transforming the Pacific Northwest. This is a place where one can forget for a moment about the dioxins and radionuclides being swept out to sea, gathering among the more than 2,000 ships that have met their demise within the rivermouth's tempestuous nexus of hidden sandbars, riptides, and storms.

Adams flouts one of the medium's cardinal rules in making this photograph—always have the sun at one's back. The bright reflection off the swirling waters almost makes the viewer squint. The image is alive with motion, light, and space, and the horizon line is slightly tilted, making the scene all the more palpable. In an influential career extending back more than thirty years, Adams' poetic, at times disturbing, documentation of the contemporary West has influenced a generation of photographers into drawing fresh attention to our place on the land.

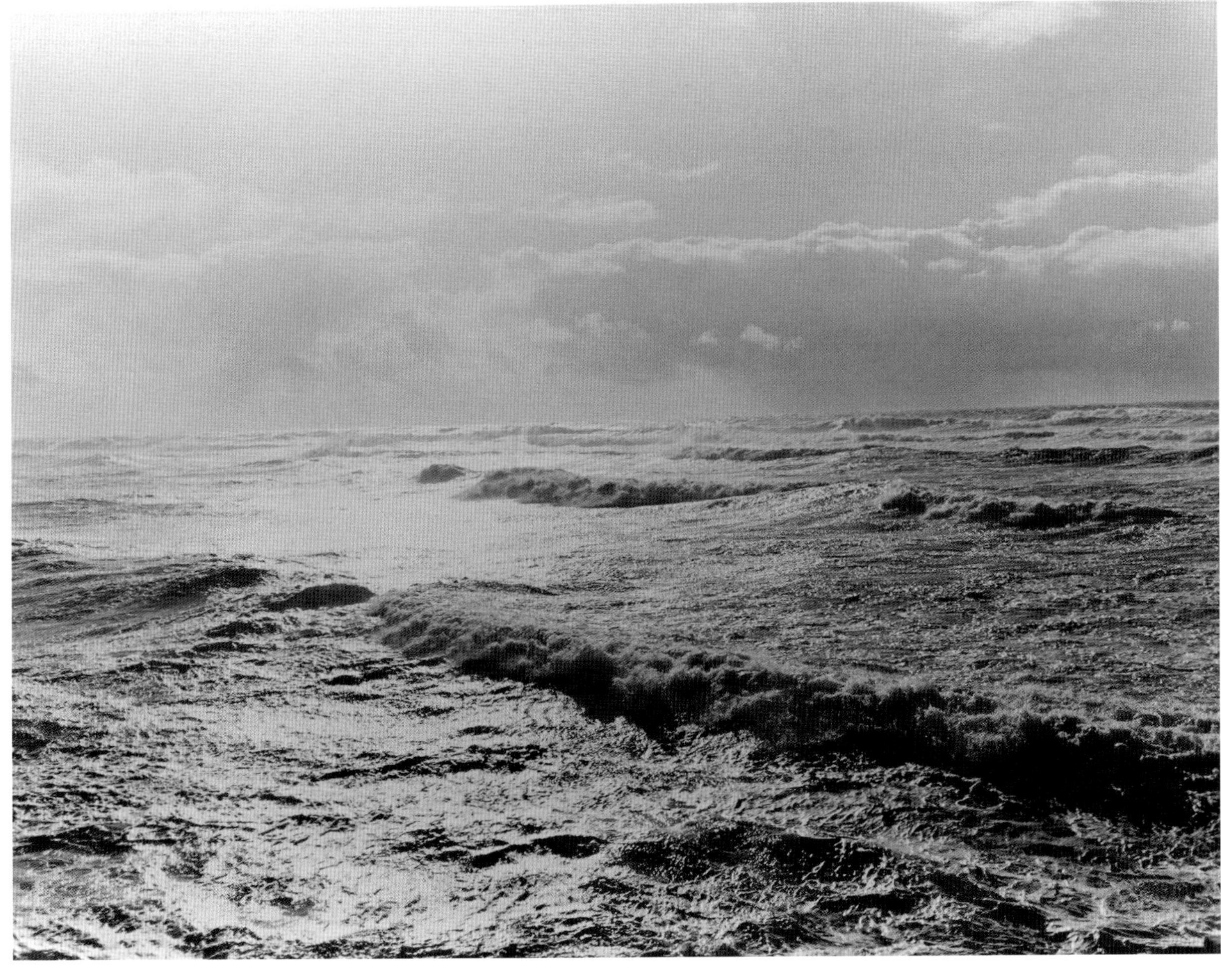

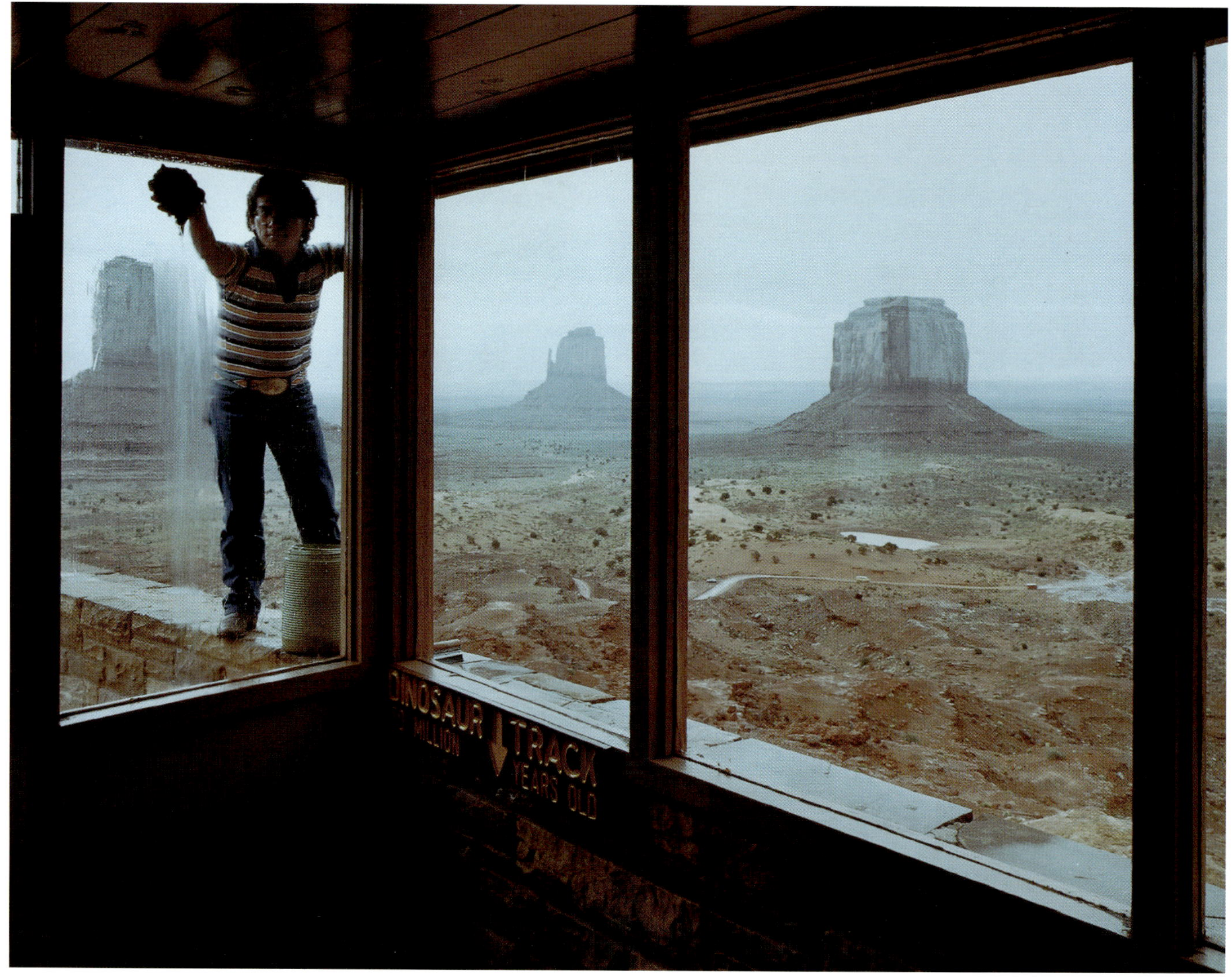

Skeet McAuley (b. 1951)

Navajo Window Washer, Monument Valley Tribal Park, Arizona, 1984
Dye destruction print
15¾ x 19¾ in. (40 x 50.2 cm)
Copyright 1983, Skeet McAuley
P1989.21.3

An American icon immortalized by painters, photographers, and movie Westerns, Monument Valley, Arizona, is instantly recognizable worldwide. Part of the Navajo reservation, the valley's towering landmarks are the lava throats of what once were mountains, now washed away over the eons. Long the subject of painters and photographers, the valley has been used time and again as a backdrop for Hollywood films dramatizing the Anglo myth of the Old West, which usually culminates in the defeat of a hostile native tribe.

This elegant, highly detailed dye destruction image is from Skeet McAuley's early-1980s series and publication, *Sign Language*, in which the photographer depicted cultural adaptations and the ironic marriage of modernity and tradition. The park employee in this photograph belongs to an ancient and proud heritage, yet he performs the everyday, mundane task of washing windows. McAuley searches for the incongruity to be found in deliberate juxtapositions of old and new, capturing an insightful glimpse of reservation life woven into the modern American lifestyle.

Native peoples first named the valley Tse Bii'nidzisgai (or White Rocks Inside), and their legends say monsters occupied the area long ago. McAuley's photograph evokes the mysteries—real or otherwise—of such a primeval landscape: the sign in the lower foreground directs the tourist's attention to a preserved track, millions of years old, that is evidence of the dinosaurs that once roamed the terrain.

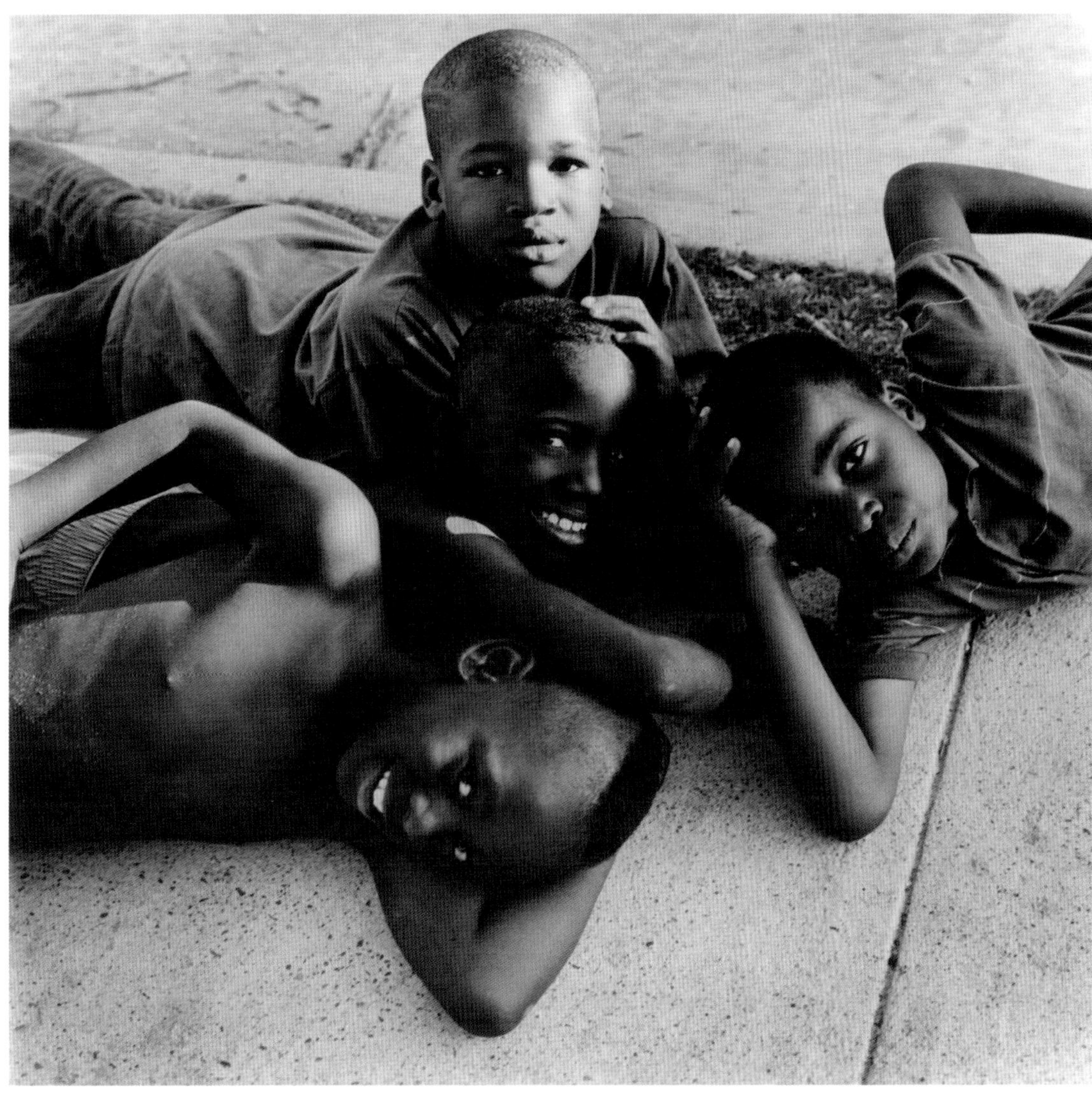

Earlie Hudnall Jr. (b. 1946)

Wheels, 1993, print 1997
Gelatin silver print
14⅞ x 15 in. (37.8 x 38.1 cm)
Copyright 1993, Earlie Hudnall Jr.
P1997.19

Earlie Hudnall Jr. grew up in Hattiesburg, Mississippi, where he developed an appreciation for personal history through his grandmother, who passed on to him stories of family and community as they sat together on the porch in the summertime. Years later, while majoring in art at Texas Southern University in Houston, the photographer received further encouragement to draw on his own experience from the artist John Biggers, who had founded the college's art department and urged his students to explore their African-American heritage. As the school yearbook editor, Hudnall went out into the community to document the daily lives of the people in the wards of Houston.

During hot summer evenings, residents of the predominantly African-American Third Ward area frequently congregate on their front porches to catch the evening breezes. This neighborhood intimacy reminded Hudnall of the sense of community he had known as a boy in Hattiesburg. He enjoyed photographing people outside, talking with their neighbors. Spotting a group of young boys huddled over a typewriter, he stopped to talk to them. After he photographed the group immersed in this activity, they asked if he would take another one of them and posed themselves in this semicircular composition. When Hudnall showed this picture to his friend Biggers, the elder artist remarked that the boys instinctively referred to their close bonds by forming a wheel with their bodies.

Further Readings about the Photography Collection

Adams, Robert. *West from the Columbia: Views at the River Mouth.* New York: Aperture, 1995.

Bruce, Roger R., ed. *Seeing the Unseen: Dr. Harold E. Edgerton and the Wonders of Strobe Alley.* Rochester, N.Y.: Publishing Trust of George Eastman House, 1994.

Cardozo, Christopher, ed. *Sacred Legacy, Edward S. Curtis and the North American Indian.* New York: Simon and Schuster, 2000.

Chiarenza, Carl. *Aaron Siskind: Pleasures and Terrors.* Boston: Little, Brown in association with Center for Creative Photography, 1982.

Davis, Keith F. *An American Century of Photography: From Dry-Plate to Digital.* 2d ed. Kansas City, Mo.: Hallmark Cards in association with Harry N. Abrams, 1999.

———. *George N. Barnard: Photographer of Sherman's Campaign.* Kansas City, Mo.: Hallmark Cards, 1990.

Dines, Elaine, ed. *Paul Outerbridge, A Singular Aesthetic: Photographs & Drawings, 1921–1941.* Laguna Beach, Calif.: Laguna Beach Museum of Art; Santa Barbara: Arabesque Books, 1981.

Dingus, Rick. *The Photographic Artifacts of Timothy O'Sullivan.* Albuquerque: University of New Mexico Press, 1982.

Fleming, Paula, and Judith Luskey. *The North American Indian in Early Photographs.* New York: Harper and Row, 1986.

Galassi, Peter. *Roy DeCarava: A Retrospective.* New York: Museum of Modern Art, 1996.

Greenough, Sarah. *Modern Art and America: Alfred Stieglitz and His New York Galleries.* Boston: Bulfinch Press, 2001.

———. *Paul Strand: An American Vision.* New York: Aperture in association with National Gallery of Art, 1990.

Hales, Peter B. *William Henry Jackson and the Transformation of the American Landscape.* Philadelphia: Temple University Press, 1988.

Hambourg, Maria Morris, et al. *Walker Evans.* New York: Metropolitan Museum of Art in association with Princeton University Press, 2000.

Junker, Patti, et al. *An American Collection: Works from the Amon Carter Museum.* New York: Hudson Hills Press in association with Amon Carter Museum, 2001.

Ketchum, Robert Glenn. *The Legacy of Wildness: The Photographs of Robert Glenn Ketchum.* New York: Aperture, 1993.

McAuley, Skeet, et al. *Sign Language: Contemporary Southwest Native America,* New York: Aperture, 1989.

McCabe, Mary Kennedy. *Clara Sipprell, Pictorial Photographer.* Fort Worth: Amon Carter Museum, 1990.

McCandless, Barbara, et al. *New York to Hollywood: The Photography of Karl Struss.* Albuquerque: University of New Mexico Press; Fort Worth: Amon Carter Museum, 1995.

Morgan, Barbara. *Martha Graham, Sixteen Dances in Photographs.* Rev. ed. Dobbs Ferry, N.Y.: Morgan and Morgan, 1980.

Mydans, Carl. *Carl Mydans, Photojournalist.* New York: Harry N. Abrams, 1985.

Newhall, Beaumont. Foreword to *Dorothea Lange Looks at the American Country Woman.* Fort Worth: Amon Carter Museum; Los Angeles: Ward Ritchie Press, 1967.

Nixon, Nicholas. *Photographs from One Year.* Boston: Institute of Contemporary Art; Carmel, Calif.: Friends of Photography, 1983.

Palmquist, Peter E. *Carleton E. Watkins: Photographer of the American West.* Albuquerque: University of New Mexico Press for Amon Carter Museum, 1983.

Price, B. Byron. *Imagining the Open Range: Erwin E. Smith, Cowboy Photographer.* Fort Worth: Amon Carter Museum, 1998.

Roark, Carol E., et al. *Catalogue of the Amon Carter Museum Photography Collection.* Fort Worth: Amon Carter Museum, 1993.

Rohrbach, John, et al. *Eliot Porter: The Color of Wildness.* New York: Aperture in association with Amon Carter Museum, 2001.

Rothstein, Arthur. *Arthur Rothstein's America in Photographs, 1930–1980.* New York: Dover Publications, 1984.

Sandweiss, Martha A. *Carlotta Corpron: Designer with Light.* Austin: University of Texas Press for Amon Carter Museum, 1980.

———. *Laura Gilpin: An Enduring Grace.* Fort Worth: Amon Carter Museum, 1986.

———, et al. *Eyewitness to War: Prints and Daguerreotypes of the Mexican War, 1846–1848.* Fort Worth: Amon Carter Museum; Washington, D.C.: Smithsonian Institution Press, 1989.

———, ed. *Photography in Nineteenth-Century America.* Fort Worth: Amon Carter Museum; New York: Harry N. Abrams, 1991.

Stebbins, Theodore E., Jr., et al. *Edward Weston: Photography and Modernism.* Boston: Museum of Fine Arts in association with Bulfinch Press, 1999.

Steichen, Joanna, ed. *Steichen's Legacy, Photographs, 1895–1973.* New York: Alfred A. Knopf, 2000.

Steinorth, Karl, ed. *Alvin Langdon Coburn: Photographs, 1900–1924.* Zurich: Edition Stemmle, 1998.

Wheeler, George M. *Wheeler's Photographic Survey of the American West, 1871–1873.* New York: Dover Publications, 1983.

Yochelson, Bonnie. *Berenice Abbott's Changing New York.* New York: New Press for Museum of the City of New York, 1997.